DYLAN THOMAS

Dylan Thomas

WALFORD DAVIES

CARDIFF
UNIVERSITY OF WALES PRESS 1990

© University of Wales and the Welsh Arts Council 1990

British Library Cataloguing in Publication Data

Davies, Walford
  Dylan Thomas.
  1. Poetry in English. Thomas, Dylan
  I. Title
  821.912

  ISBN 0-7083-1066-4

All rights reserved. No part of this book may be reproduced, stored in a retrieval system, or transmitted, in any form or by any means, electronic, mechanical, photocopying, recording or otherwise, without clearance from the University of Wales Press, 6 Gwennyth Street, Cardiff CF2 4YD.

Typeset in Wales by Afal, Cardiff
Designed in Wales by Cloud Nine, Cardiff
Printed in Wales by Gwasg John Penry, Swansea

Preface

Once it was the colour of saying
Soaked my table the uglier side of a hill . . .

Now my saying shall be my undoing,
And every stone I wind off like a reel.

The opportunity to travel back through time to reclaim and reconsider something said or done — or left *unsaid* or *undone* — seems appropriate to the very nature of Dylan Thomas's work. He is, after all, a writer much possessed by time, as also by redeeming memory. In a late Wordsworth sonnet ('Mutability') a magical phrase concerning the very nature of time — 'the unimaginable touch of Time' — seems all the more poignant for being itself a phrase salvaged by Wordsworth from a much earlier, abandoned work. In the same way, Dylan Thomas often found himself going back and issuing or reissuing part or parts of an earlier self, from an individual phrase to a complete poem, from an isolated memory to a complete childhood. All the while, however, his artist's and craftsman's instinct for the need to develop, and to fare forward, remained strong. The opening and the closing of his 1938 poem 'Once it was the colour of saying', quoted above, show the poet's concern to allow the exercise of going back ('*Once it was . . .*') to be the means of going forward ('*Now . . . shall be . . .*').

A critic engaged on an analogous exercise — asked, in this case, to consider the reissue of a study written close on twenty years ago — is bound to be intrigued by at least one question. How radically different would this essay be if I were writing it now? On that score, I am pleased to find that I would want to stand by most of what is claimed or argued here. Of course, the relatively short compass allowed by the aims and format of the Writers of Wales Series, for which the original study was commissioned by the Welsh Arts

Council, makes one feel that greater elbow-room would have been a welcome help in more firmly establishing some of the points made. In particular, I would have welcomed the opportunity to expand the comparisons and contrasts drawn between Thomas and his English contemporaries, along with the cultural and sociological significance of the reaction that set in against the poet after his premature death in the early 1950s. But, on the other hand, the relative restriction of the series' brief and format encouraged from the beginning a salutary concentration on what essentially characterizes Thomas as a 'writer of Wales'. Republishing the study now, I remain convinced that the true patterns of Thomas's powers (and, by the same token, of his limitations) are always meaningfully traced back to that basic fact of his Welshness.

The reissue of the volume has, however, given me the opportunity of making a few changes and additions. Greater clarity dictated the need for the changes, and the criterion of critical usefulness determined the additions. In both, I am indebted to my sons Jason and Damian: born in the year in which this book was written (1971), and now aged nineteen at its reissue, they are to be thanked for telling me so clearly what needed explanation and expansion.

April 1990   *Walford Davies*

NOTE

The quotations from Dylan Thomas's poetry are made from the corrected text established in the new *Dylan Thomas: Collected Poems 1934–1953*, edited by Walford Davies and Ralph Maud (London: Dent, 1988).

The cover photograph, showing the poet at the age of nineteen in 1933, is suitably chosen. Too often Dylan Thomas, like Wordsworth, is celebrated in portraits reflecting a later self instead of the younger face behind earlier (if anything, more phenomenal) years of achievement. A trick of perspective in a now famous 1952 photograph in Laugharne churchyard, eerily merging a lionized poet with graves and undergrowth (only a few yards, as it happens, from where he was himself to be buried), or the expected photographic stance at pint-tables and lecture-rostrums — these speak of a poet keeping abreast of a legend. Further back lies another impression — that of a sensitive provincial adolescent dangerously aware of a verbal talent which might indeed some day make a legend, reassuring his mother that one day he would be 'better than Keats'.

This way, we can have it both ways. We can emphasize a gauche adolescence, trapped by ordinariness, and still concede the glamorizing self-regard of a young man who sensed — early and justifiably — that he could write. The defensive remark about Keats was made because his mother wondered whether Thomas, apparently idling at home, should not be following the usual route to the university: 'Anybody'd think you were a Keats or something,' she'd taunted. And in sympathizing with him, we need not submit to the seductive notion of a mere 'woodnotes wild' precocity. The tones in which the poet later described his limited formal education — 'demure, chequered' — are certainly not injured ones. In any case, Swansea Grammar School, which he attended from 1925 to 1931, and where his father was Senior English Master, had had a liberal take-it-or-leave-it regime that enabled him usefully to help himself. A former Classics master recorded that Thomas at one stage 'wanted to hear a bit of Vergil, though I don't think he was a

Latin scholar at all. He came for about two months, until it was time to edit the magazine, and then I didn't see him any more.' But, more important, it is clear to the critical reader — as all along it was certainly clear to intimate friends — that here was a tough intelligence which was not betrayed by being independent of intellectual discipline, ideological commitment, or philosophical 'knowingness'. His relationship to the modern and contemporary lions of the English poetic tradition remained much like that of Keats to Wordsworth and Coleridge: he was impressed, but also mistrusted some of the wider intellectual implications of their art. The analogy is with the young Keats's mistrust of Wordsworth's 'egotistical sublime', of poetry that 'has a palpable design upon us'. Not for Thomas the cultural memory of T.S. Eliot (whom he dubbed 'Pope Eliot') or the collective political/poetic programmes of Auden's circle ('Congratulations on Auden's seventieth birthday,' he quipped — in 1937, when Auden was only thirty!). And there remains a clear difference between, say, Thomas's vague alignment with Freud —

> Freud cast light on a little of the darkness he had exposed. Benefiting by the sight of the light and the knowledge of the hidden nakedness, poetry must drag further into the clean nakedness of light more even of the hidden causes than Freud could realise
>
> ('Answers to an Enquiry', 1934) —

and Auden's *use* of Freud. At the stage when a period at university might have disciplined Thomas's haphazard reading and invited him (in Coleridge's phrase) 'to generalize his notions', he remained at home, often sickly and much pampered by his mother, committing poems to the private storehouse of school exercise-books (the type with arithmetic tables and 'Danger-Don'ts' on the back), the now famous poetry Notebooks.

In reintroducing him in a Welsh context, however, we have to bear in mind that his perspectives were always bound to be wider than that domestic or provincial context, because his primary allegiance was to the English language itself — the only one he knew:

> The bad influences I tried to remove and renounce bit by bit, shadow by shadow, echo by echo, through trial and error, through delight and

2

disgust and misgiving, as I came to love words more and to hate the heavy hands that knocked them about, the thick tongues that had no feel for their multitudinous tastes, the dull and botching hacks who flattened them out into a colourless and insipid paste, the pedants who made them moribund and pompous as themselves.

('Poetic Manifesto', 1951)

It is not invariably true, either, that 'A penny life will give you all the facts', especially in a case like Thomas's, where the pattern seems to have been often almost comically mundane. Suburban boredom, self-conscious bohemian release, first of all in the Kardomah Café and the pubs of Swansea (his 'Little Dublin') and then in Soho, strenuous financial survival throughout, an America which did to his every word what the poet did to their liquor: these see us through from Swansea to London to New York, taught the poet no radically new habits of thought or action, and shaped the routine even in Laugharne where he was most at ease, and finally at rest. But they take us through, also, from the difficult stylistic and thematic originality of the early poems to the dense and driven passion of the elegies on London's wartime dead, to the melodramatic facility of the film-scripts or the comic facility of the broadcasts, to the pastoral emphasis of the later poetry and the final elegiac cartoon of Welsh life in *Under Milk Wood*, the 'Play for Voices'. The pleasure of literary criticism is that it invites us to trust more readily the poem than the poet, the artefacts rather than the 'facts' — a welcome relief in this case, since the boozy legend of the life has loomed so large. But it is worth noting that, where biography is the aim, the approach to Constantine FitzGibbon's *The Life of Dylan Thomas* (1965) is more penetrating by being also more sympathetic than, say, the snapshots in a vacuum of John Malcolm Brinnin's *Dylan Thomas in America* (1955). And a similar point may be registered on the critical side. We will not be attending to the matter in hand if, favouring different ways with words than those which intrigued Thomas, or sharing the ironic reflexes of the new generation of poets who succeeded and reacted against Thomas in the fifties and sixties, we start from suspicion; nor if, loving Wales herself too well, we expect that only one kind of tribute can be paid her. Dylan Thomas knew only one conscious allegiance — that to his 'craft and sullen art'. Attending to it, we reaffirm the truth of

Yeats's dictum that the poet who writes the poem is never merely the bundle of accidents and incoherence that sat down to breakfast. Indeed, in the presence of FitzGibbon's admirable *Life* — and of its even more capacious and accurate (if less sympathetic) successor, Paul Ferris's *Dylan Thomas* (1977) — much of the burden of biographical detail ('the penny facts') is taken off this essay. It will be enough to keep our chronological bearings and highlight only such attitudes and responses as lie *behind* the 'facts' and bear on an understanding of the work itself.

The question, for example, of Dylan Thomas's parents. The English-speaking suburban home in Swansea into which the poet was born (27 October 1914) had deeper and wider roots. His father, who exerted the greatest single influence on Thomas's early years, and his mother, a kindly woman who came nevertheless to symbolize for him the quality of Welsh suburban triviality, relayed unconsciously another and older culture into his life. Both parents had sprung from working-class, rural and Welsh-speaking beginnings in Carmarthenshire, though these roots had been most effectively overlaid by the kind of life they had consolidated at No.5 Cwmdonkin Drive (the young Dylan's 'Glamorgan villa') with its neo-Georgian respectability, its middle-class decorative gestures in knitted texts and reproduction Greek statues, and its resident maid. David John Thomas, the Grammar School senior English master who presided over this home, was also — and probably for the same motives — the man who, within that home, had deliberately suppressed his own native Welsh language and erased the further bogy of a Welsh accent by ensuring that his son and daughter received elocution lessons. (For a certain class in the Swansea of that day, English elocution lessons were a fashionable phenomenon.) The cut-glass accent of the voice which was to be almost the most attractive aspect of the later 'legend' was therefore of an early, and defensive, manufacture — and the father's motive in the whole matter would have had something to do, no doubt, with the idea of 'getting on in the world'.

The irony of this hiatus in a purely Welsh lineage can be marked for our purposes by the mention of D.J. Thomas's uncle, William Thomas (1834–79) whose poetic name, Gwilym Marles, gave Dylan Thomas his middle name of Marlais. Born in Carmarthenshire, this preacher-poet had been in effect the father of modern

4

Unitarianism in Wales and a passionate and radical agitator in the landlord-tenant friction which followed the wider franchise of the Reform Bill of 1867. His whole personality and the character of his brief life were such as could not be divorced from the nature of a radical, Welsh-speaking, rural community, and from the properties of the Welsh language itself. Though probably only a shadowy figure in Dylan Thomas's own awareness, his eminence in terms of family and national life must have loomed large in D.J. Thomas's consciousness, and the break with the Welsh language effected by the latter within the home seems, in this connection, even more strange, defined and resolute. A failed poet himself (and, as it happens, an unsuccessful applicant for the first Chair of English at the brand-new University College of Swansea in 1920), D.J. Thomas's greatest ambition was that such failures should be corrected a generation late, and in English. His positive, as opposed to his reactionary, influences in that direction were clearly salutary: his fine reading voice, his decision that the young Dylan's acquaintance with especially the verse of Shakespeare should not have to await intellectual maturity, and his discriminating taste also in modern writers (notably Edward Thomas and D.H. Lawrence) redress somewhat the balance of our first impressions. Indeed, it is possible that the emotional distance between the poet and his severe, often disgruntled, father during the early years accidentally made Thomas more readily appreciate, as if in relief, the literary enthusiasm which must have seemed D.J. Thomas's main saving grace.

From his mother's family the poet derived simpler, environmental pleasures. Her eldest sister, Annie, had married Jack Jones who farmed Fernhill outside Carmarthen, and it was there of course that Thomas, from as early as 1917, and throughout the 1920s, enjoyed those now famous schoolboy holidays, celebrated in the story 'The Peaches' and the poem 'Fern Hill'. Another aunt married the Reverend David Rees, minister of Paraclete Congregational Chapel in Newton, Swansea, where the young boy spent a good deal of his time, exposed quite naturally to such verbal and other legacies as we normally associate with chapel and Sunday school in Wales. His mother's family were in fact the aunts and uncles of the later broadcast, 'Memories of Christmas' (1945). A photograph is reproduced in Bill Read's *The Days of Dylan Thomas* (p.64) which shows some of these relatives standing with Pamela Hansford Johnson, the poet and novelist whose copious correspondence with Dylan Thomas between 1933 and 1935 helped him to articulate his sensibility outside the poems and train his sights on literary London. Nothing could register more graphically than that 1936 photograph the poet's position half-way between thoroughly Welsh, rural beginnings and later London fame.

So what about that Welsh-speaking tradition which seems to have been so consciously denied him at source? Could it still have exerted an influence? Talk about 'modified *cynghanedd*' seems futile in the case of a poet who would presumably have been hard pressed to identify, let alone modify, it. It seems reasonable to suggest that a primarily Welsh-speaking poet will use the English language more idiosyncratically than a writer more comfortably locked inside English idioms. The imaginative freedoms of the *métèque* (that is to say, the writer with a non-English linguistic, racial or political background) are possible because the habituating tendencies of those English idioms are at some distance from his consciousness and a certain objectivity (and consequently adventurousness) proves possible. The case of a Welsh-speaking writer is interesting also in as much as, in him, the idiosyncracy is uncompromising because also unconscious. But we will have to curtail that precise argument, of course, because Dylan Thomas spoke no Welsh, so that nothing would seem necessarily to have pushed him towards deviation from English idiomatic, syntactic, or stylistic norms. But returning to the point, we can gauge alternative explanations.

First, it is likely that the privacy of Thomas's early Notebooks, written in a provincial town, and in Wales (circles within circles), ensured a kind of literary *laissez-faire* which a more obviously advantaged and fashionable London context, for example, would not have prompted. In this sense, Gerard Manley Hopkins, the obscure Victorian Jesuit, or the reclusive Emily Dickinson in mid nineteenth-century New England, offer more extreme parallels in terms of the privacy in which their wilful major poetry was produced. They could afford to explore eccentric styles and visions away from the centre and in the absence of any large public audience that would have demanded orthodoxy in such matters. (But, of course, Hopkins was further influenced in that direction from 1874 onwards by virtue of his learning Welsh, and reading Welsh strict-metre poetry.) Secondly, it strikes me that Constantine FitzGibbon minimizes the significance of Thomas's non-Welsh-speaking status in the right way when he says in his *Life* that 'because the English words and syntax do not always and exactly fit the ideas and images to be expressed, the recently anglicized "Celt" will examine his language with a very close attention'. This survival of a radically Welsh mode of thought or sensibility beyond the Anglicization of a second generation is of course difficult to prove: it is just that we feel its palpable manifestation to be there, and beyond argument. Agreement on this point is urged, not only by the linguistic texture of the verse, but also by incidental evidence which in another context might appear innocent. For example Thomas kept a private dictionary of favourite words, suggesting something of an outsider's interest in their potentialities:

> The greatest single word I know is 'drome' which, for some reason, nearly opens the doors of heaven for me. Say it yourself, out aloud, and see if you can hear the golden gates swing backward as the last, long sound of the 'm' fades away.
>
> (Letter to Pamela Hansford Johnson, 1933)

And in a restaurant one day he was immoderately excited by the discovery that 'live' spelt 'evil' backwards.

A third explanation of the phenomenon is a related and again a collectively psychological one. A Welshman, it seems fair to argue, whether he speaks Welsh or not, has ingrained in him a certain view of his art — a kind of collective sense of his responsibility towards form. Again the survival of a cultural temperament, this attitude exists on both sides of the Welsh-language barrier, and is itself in turn a barrier against intrusion from other cultures, certainly in the matter of literary assumptions. This is interesting in Dylan Thomas's case because of his general admiration for his English counterparts. The poetry of his English contemporaries had already been influenced by Eliot and Pound's concern 'to purify the dialect of the tribe' and was in the process of being further influenced by what one might call Audenese — the assumption of a thin-lipped articulateness which turned on irony and understatement and was marked, often at the expense of feeling, by cold intelligence. Thomas's commitment to the reverse was profound, and should not be undervalued simply because of the jocular way in which he often tended to express that commitment outside his poems. In 'On Reading One's Own Poems' (broadcast 1949) he found alien symptoms in even the way some English poets read their verse aloud. Thomas speaks of the poet

> who manages, by studious flatness, semi-detachment, and an almost condescending undersaying of his poems, to give the impression that what he really means is: Great things, but my own.

As with the delivery, so with the making. A Welshman, with this natural resistance to the anti-poetic, wanted (as John Wain once put it) a poem to look like a poem, and to sound like poetry, not like conversation overheard. It is a parallel achievement of W.B. Yeats's that he should have retained a musical, Celtic resonance while at the same time giving way to the measure of colloquial hardness he assumed on the advice of Ezra Pound. In this sense, modern English poetry in Wales probably also continued to have a natural resistance to, say, the post-1950s influence of something like Charles Olson's 'Projective Verse' poetic, in which poems are structured by natural 'voice' projections rather than by an objective view of the poem's shape and pattern on the page. And if later Anglo-Welsh poets have found Dylan Thomas in specifically verbal and formal matters too rich, too arch, it is also probably because, from R.S. Thomas onwards, they have got down more closely to the realistic details of Welsh life than Dylan Thomas ever did, and in the face of rural depopulation, urban unemployment and bombed dams the verbal gestures have to be suitably chastened.

But our immediate concern is what things looked like to a young Swansea poet in the thirties, when the larger issues which his poetry, at least, chose to ignore — poverty, unemployment, a sense of Europe — were as obvious in Swansea as they were in Oxford, London or Birmingham. These things might well have tempted him to intellectualize his voice. But the young man who wrote like this —

> Awake, my sleeper, to the sun,
> A worker in the morning town,
> And leave the poppied pickthank where he lies;
> The fences of the light are down,
> All but the briskest riders thrown,
> And worlds hang on the trees —

must have done so because he did not wish to write like this:

> The live ones are
> Those who, going to work early, behold the world's
> Utter margin where all is stone and iron,
> And wrong. While the dead sleep
> The bins are emptied, the streets washed of their dung,
> The first trucks shunted; and the will emerges
> On alteration.

(Stephen Spender's Vienna, 1934)

The Thomas quotation is the last stanza of 'When once the twilight locks' (1934). The presence in both quotations of that image of the proletarian early-riser only serves to highlight the radical difference between these two contemporary poets in terms of texture, shape and sound. I quote Spender's *Vienna* conveniently, because in December 1934 Thomas reviewed that very poem in *New Verse*. Though he does not actually quote from the poem, Thomas in his review registered the kind of aesthetic shock he experienced on reading it:

> There is more than poetry in poems, in that much even of the most considerable poem is unpoetical or anti-poetical, is dependent upon the wit that discovers occult resemblances in things apparently unlike or upon the intellectual consciousness of the necessity for a social conscience. In a poem, however, the poetry must come first; what negates or acts against the poem must be subjugated to the poetry which is essentially indifferent to whatever philosophy, political passion, or gang-belief it embraces ... As a poem, *Vienna* leaves much to be desired; in the first place it leaves poetry to be desired.

Four months before, in another review of contemporary poetry, printed in the *Adelphi*, he had rounded on poets as different as Auden and Day Lewis on the one hand, and Pound, Ronald Bottrall and William Carlos Williams on the other, in these terms:

> 'The Death of the Ear' would be an apt subtitle for a book on the plight of modern poetry ... Too much poetry today is flat on the page, a black and white thing of words created by intelligences that no longer think it necessary for a poem to be read and understood by anything but the eyes.

It need not be emphasized here that no response as sweeping as this will be in any way fair to the best of the poets mentioned. In any case, Thomas himself came to suffer from equally summary judgements: the world of literary reputations brings in its own revenges. But we cannot but admire the decisiveness of the response, and the no-nonsense urgency of its expression. Like every other poet, the young Thomas felt the need to help create the taste by which his own poetry was to be enjoyed. And integral to a taste for Thomas's poetry is an acceptance of its formal delights and musical necessities. This is what William Empson, the most distinguished and enthusiastic of Thomas's advocates, had in mind when he used to say of many a maligned poet — Thomas included — 'But surely, he has the root of the matter in him! He has a singing line!' Thomas's occasional criticism shows him holding out against the demythologization of the world of poetry as it might threaten the appropriately 'Celtic' role of form and sound in the creation of memorable speech.

And yet after the largely parodic juvenilia with which, between 1925 and 1931, he had made the *Swansea Grammar School Magazine* almost a personal forum, Thomas's first gropings towards something like an individual voice seem to have been an attempt first of all at formal freedom. The bulk of the first three of his four extant poetry Notebooks (1930-3) was of what he called 'Mainly Free Verse Poems', suggesting an easy acceptance of a 'liberating' modernism he would have associated variously with the Imagists, the Sitwells or with Eliot. But this bulk is also strangely thick-ankled and rather murkily confessional, as may be seen in Ralph Maud's edition of the Notebooks, *Poet in the Making* (1968, 2nd ed. 1989). A prosaic casualness did not quite suit Thomas. For example:

> When all your tunes have caused
> The pianola's roll to break,
> And, no longer young but careful,
> There are no words by which you might express
> The thoughts you seem to let go by,
> You might consider me . . .

> (Poem '36', 1930 Notebook)

Eschewing stricter forms (or 'water-tight columns' of words, as he later called them) in these earlier Notebook poems meant that the only tension came from the local excitement of image and symbol. A Modernist delight in writing imagistically survived, in fact, until well over the half-way mark of Thomas's career. But it also came to approximate more to Symbolist than to Imagist technique. That is to say, the images came to have, as it were, a narrative life of their own, and the quality of statement (and the modicum of descriptive intent that even Imagism allowed) fell away. Thomas had later to beg even Edith Sitwell to read the 'Altarwise by owl-light' sonnets 'literally' — that is, without weaving an imported paraphrase around the literal narrative.

And as Thomas came more and more to distrust any casually discursive or moralistic voice in poetry, other formal properties also came to provide the *frisson* of the verse, notably a growing tendency towards half-rhymed stanzaic forms and tighter incantational or repetitive patterns. In the third Notebook (February–August 1933), therefore, a casual emotional honesty gave way to a chiselling craft which set welcome obstacles in the way of the voice's incantational resonance. The magnificent 'Before I knocked' (1933), for example, sustains no fewer than twenty-three percussive rhymes ending in 'er'; while in 'I, in my intricate image' (1935), seventy-two lines close with words ending somehow on the letter 'I'. Thomas uttered lamenting asides throughout his career about the expensive demands made by such formal energy. But if we imagine that the strain was broken in the apparently more dilute later verse, we should remind ourselves of the careful internal rhymes of 'The conversation of prayers' (1945), the patterned image organization of 'Fern Hill' (1945), the beautifully handled villanelle form of 'Do not go gentle into that good night' (finished 1951), the unbroken syllabic-counts (6, 9, 6, 9, 6, 9, 6, 9, 6) of the lines within each stanza of 'Poem on his Birthday' (finished 1951) and the fantastic rhyme-scheme of 'Prologue' (1952). In that 102-line 'Prologue', the first and last lines rhyme, and so on inwards until the exact centre of the poem is a rhyming couplet. This last example shows more clearly than any the calculated obstacle-race quality of Thomas's mode of composition. A nation to whom *englynion* and *cynghanedd*, however strenuously achieved, seem as much art as craft is in the end right in recognizing in Thomas one of her own. And if the salute is required to be evaluative as well as nepotist, I would add that such hard-earned memorability in poetry has tended, during four decades of 'Dylan-baiting', to be wrongly devalued as an affective, aesthetic pleasure.

Our amazement at the virtuosity of the poet accommodating the diamond and hour-glass shapes of 'Vision and Prayer' (1944) is our initiation into its experience, eliciting a deeper response than cool paraphrase. But, of course, this tendency to shape a naturally expansive voice across or within wilful verbal patterns can only be praised or blamed on its end-results. It is, presumably, no disqualification of Gerard Manley Hopkins's wonderful sonnet 'The Starlight Night', for example, to have it pointed out that in that freshly expressive poem Hopkins has in fact clustered his images alphabetically!

> Look at the stars! look, look up at the skies!
>   O look at all the fire-folk sitting in the air!
>   The bright boroughs, the circle-citadels there!
> Down in dim woods the diamond delves! the elves'-eyes!
> The grey lawns cold where gold, where quickgold lies!
>   Wind-beat whitebeam! airy abeles set on a flare!
> Flake-doves sent floating forth at a farmyard scare!

It was natural for the linguist and classical prosodist in Hopkins to become interested in Welsh-language strict-metre poetics. Thomas, less academically curious perhaps, was already temperamentally inside the Celtic tradition of the poet as maker. And from his father, and an early friend such as Glyn Jones or a later friend such as Aneirin Talfan Davies, he would have learned even about the Welsh strict-metre tradition itself; certainly as much as suited his own, quite resolute purposes. The syllabic rigour of 'In my craft or sullen art' (1945) adds self-referential force to that poem's assertion that 'I *labour* by singing light'. The poem insists that poetry is a craft: or, if an art, a *sullen* art. For this Welshman, if poetry had had (in Keats's phrase) to come 'as naturally as leaves to a tree', it would not have come at all.

But to think of Wales is to be also reminded specifically, in this case, of Swansea. And more useful than any strict biographical detail in retracing our steps is the imaginative autobiography of *Portrait of the Artist as a Young Dog*, the collection of short stories which the poet wrote, with some measure of amused perspective, between 1938 and 1940. These stories colourfully register all that Swansea meant to the young poet in retrospect: the urchin adventures, the loved ordinariness of the familiar, the bourgeois Nonconformist norms, the paradox of an industrial area skirted by its pastoral or seaside opposites, miniature bohemian freedom over coffee in the 'Kardomah', and the private hopes of escaping a life-at-siege through an insistence on the fact that the young dog was also an artist. The *Portrait* is valuable as a piece of atmospheric impressionism, truer than any total recall or mere reportage could ever be. It distils the kind of instinctual Welshness which Thomas could still unerringly catch even in his very last short story (the one about the charabanc outing, written in 1953) or in *Under Milk Wood*. Cool sociologizing would have been the death of all three.

A section from the story called 'A Fight' will illustrate the *Portrait*'s crisp appeal. Thomas is re-creating an evening at the home of his closest schoolboy friend, Daniel Jones:

'What were you talking to Mr Morris about in the street, Dad?' asked Dan. 'We saw you from upstairs.'

'I was telling him how the Swansea and District Male Voice did the *Messiah*, that's all. Why do you ask?'

Mr Bevan couldn't eat any more, he was full. For the first time since supper began, he looked round the table. He didn't seem to like what he saw. 'How are studies progressing, Daniel?'

'Listen to Mr Bevan, Dan, he's asking you a question.'

'Oh, so so.'

'So so?'

'I mean they're going very well, thank you, Mr Bevan.'

'Young people should attempt to say what they mean.'

Mrs Bevan giggled, and asked for more meat. 'More meat,' she said.

'And you, young man, have you a mathematical bent?'

'No, sir,' I said, 'I like English.'

'He's a poet,' said Dan, and looked uncomfortable.

'A brother poet,' Mr Bevan corrected, showing his teeth.

'Mr Bevan has published books,' said Mr Jenkyn. '*Proserpine, Psyche* —'

'*Orpheus*,' said Mr Bevan sharply.

'And *Orpheus*. You must show Mr Bevan some of your verses.'

'I haven't got anything with me, Mr Jenkyn.'

'A poet,' said Mr Bevan, 'should carry his verses in his head.'

'I remember them all right,' I said.

'Recite me your latest one; I'm always very interested.'

'What a gathering,' Mrs Jenkyn said, 'poets, musicians, preachers. We only want a painter now, don't we?'

'I don't think you'll like the very latest one,' I said.

'Perhaps', said Mr Bevan, smiling, 'I am the best judge of that.'

'Frivolous is my hate,' I said, wanting to die, watching Mr Bevan's teeth.

> 'Singed with bestial remorse,
> Of unfulfilment of desired force,
> And lust of tearing late;
>
> 'Now could I raise
> Her dead, dark body to my own
> And hear the joyous rustle of her bone
> And in her eyes see deathly blaze;
>
> 'Now could I wake
> To passion after death, and taste
> The rapture of her hating, tear the waste
> Of body. Break, her dead, dark body, break.'

Dan kicked my shins in the silence before Mr Bevan said: 'The influence is obvious of course. "Break, break, break, on thy cold, grey stones, O sea." '

'Hubert knows Tennyson backwards,' said Mrs Bevan, 'backwards.'

But the tone had not always been this one of comic remove. Far from it. The young man who actually wrote such great poems of adolescent sexual awakening as 'The force that through the green fuse' (1933) and 'If I were tickled by the rub of love' (1934) had, in his letters, consistently struck a distinctly *uncomic* note before literary London gave him that escape-ticket from his 'Little Dublin'. Writing to Geoffrey Grigson, then editor of the highly influential *New Verse*, in 1933 for example:

> I have developed, intellectually at least, in the smug darkness of a provincial town . . . Grinding out poetry, whether good or bad, in such an atmosphere as surrounds me, is depressing and disheartening.

Thomas left Swansea Grammar School in the summer of 1931. He first went to live in London in November 1934, when he was twenty. The period in between was his most prolific, and in some ways the most genuinely 'marvellous'. The personal voice which it established disturbed the cosmopolitan literary scene with his first mature London publication, 'And death shall have no dominion', which appeared in the *New English Weekly* in May 1933. He made his first visit to London in the summer of that year. Several other visits, but mainly his contribution of poems like 'The force that through the green fuse' to a reputable newspaper called *The Sunday Referee*, earned him his first volume, *18 Poems*, published in December 1934. The 'Poets' Corner' of *The Sunday Referee* had decided to award the major prize of a first-volume publication to the best contributor. That its critical judgement in such matters was not absolutely sound is suggested by the fact that the first prize-winner of this kind was, not Thomas, but Pamela Hansford Johnson — in 1933. But that it was very close to being sound was shown by the poetry editor's particularly strong admiration for Thomas's submitted poems, and the award of the second published volume to the twenty-year-old from Swansea. Thus encouraged, Thomas's sights were set on London life and London publication for various reasons, not least amongst them a fear of being left isolated in smug, provincial obscurity. Swansea friends like the artist Fred Janes and the composer Daniel Jones were leaving the town. On an even more personal level, in 1933 his father contracted cancer of the mouth, forcing him soon to resign from the Grammar School. Holidays at Fernhill no longer took place; in spring 1933, Annie Jones died. The world was closing in.

It should also be mentioned that the poet's first adult employment, as a journalist on the *South Wales Daily Post* (July 1931–December 1932), had long since proved comically uncommitted. Graham Greene in his autobiography, *A Sort of Life*, has pinpointed the virtues of a journalistic apprenticeship for a certain kind of creative writer: he learns 'lessons valuable to his own craft. He is removing the clichés of reporters; he is compressing a story to the minimum length possible without ruining its effect. A writer with a sprawling style is unlikely to emerge from such an apprenticeship.' These were not necessarily lessons or virtues Thomas would have agreed with; his poetry had its own kind of discipline, and his prose never looked as if it might salute any ordinary kind of economy. The importance of his early experience of journalism lay, rather, in its exposure of the foibles and irregularities of Swansea life, later useful for *Portrait of the Artist as a Young Dog* and even, in a stored-up way, for *Under Milk Wood*.

But the real cause of his journalistic failure — an unusual incompetence in matters demanding a punctilious respect for deadlines — pointed to the later legend. The three years between school and final entry into London life made everything grist to his mill and were conducted quite unadventurously on the level of café, pub and cinema. The cinema images of so many of his early poems —

> In this our age the gunman and his moll,
> Two one-dimensioned ghosts, love on a reel,
> Strange to our solid eye,
> And speak their midnight nothings as they swell
>
> ('Our eunuch dreams', 1934) —

were not merely intellectual invention. Thomas had contributed a knowledgeable essay on 'The Films' to his school magazine in July 1930. The proverbial tell-tale signs of a 'misspent' youth were redeemed in the imaginative force of the poems' cinematic images.

Another activity during these pre-London years was equally symptomatic. Thomas was a good actor and enthusiastically played in productions at the Grand Theatre and (mainly) the Swansea Little Theatre, whose repertoire ranged from Coward's *Hay Fever* to Farquhar's *The Beaux' Stratagem*, Congreve's *The Way of the World*, and Shakespeare's *Richard II*. The resonance of his voice was already impressive, and his later quality as a broadcaster was a natural extension of a quite remarkable dramatic gift. It has become fashionable — perhaps as a recoil from something too obviously good — to decry Thomas's reading of poetry. In fact it is far more varied and interpretatively controlled than is commonly allowed, especially in his readings of other poets such as Hardy and Auden. Moreover, the weight and density of his treatment of his own words on the page probably owe a good deal to the straightforward unembarrassed resonance of his own actual speaking voice.

His Swansea activities during these years all had one thing in common — the cultivation of like-minded friends. That group was not remarkably wide and there was, even here, the formation of something like a defensive inner circle. Ethel Ross has claimed, in an examination of Thomas's acting years, that 'there was a slight aura of sin hanging over the theatre in the eyes of many Nonconformists'. And the *Mumbles Press*, reviewing a production of Rodney Ackland's *Strange Orchestra*, in which Thomas played a leading part, lamented the bringing 'into public view of those things which we normally think most decent to hide'. Thomas's assertive sense of freedom was constantly finding these resistant aspects of Swansea life a real threat.

This might suggest that from the start he lacked a genuinely anchoring context. And to some degree this would be a true impression. Certainly the Swansea he knew, and described in much the same way as Edward Thomas had seen it (a poet born there 'would have no need of Heaven or Hell'), never became objectively and contemporaneously (only retrospectively) crucial to his serious art. Despite the physical and spiritual scarring of the twenties and thirties, with their 28,000 Swansea unemployed, his unsuccessful attempts to register the situation in art had already blocked out for him one of the fashionable poetic manners of the early thirties. His test was always the technical accomplishment of a poem, not its conscience. He must therefore have seen that early Notebook poems of his which contained lines such as 'Young men with fallen chests and old men's breath' or 'The living dead left over from the war' begged ideological development such as he could not offer. And in reviews of poetry which he wrote for London periodicals in the thirties he continued to berate poets like Stephen Spender and John Pudney for setting political above literary effects. Even in the *Portrait* stories, the social malaise of that early world of unemployment is only obliquely registered — in for example the curious situation of three young men aimlessly loitering under the pier, which is the haunting image as well as the structure of the story titled 'Just Like Little Dogs'.

Very early, his view of his poetic art had a certain aesthetic base — the idea of poetry as something manufactured, as an independent, semantic world. There was an element of the professional in it too:

> I had to imitate and parody . . . consciously, or unconsciously: I had to try to learn what made words tick . . . because I wanted to write what I wanted to write before I knew how to write or what I wanted to.

In this sense his field of reference lay very much outside Swansea — in the manner, if not the matter, of an English tradition, though always subject to the Celtic regard for formal resonance which we have already noted. Of course, the schoolboy parodic tendencies did not suddenly disappear. Inside even the individual, maturing voice there remained an assimilative facility which could suggest Eliot,

> the silent tide
> Lapping the still canals, the dry tide-master
> Ribbed between desert and water storm

('We lying by seasand', 1933)

or Auden,

> Neither by night's ancient fear,
> The parting of hat from hair,
> Pursed lips at the receiver

('I have longed to move away', 1933)

or could expand the individual cadence of Wilfred Owen's line 'Foreheads of men have bled where no wounds were' into the curious framework of 'Light breaks where no sun shines' (1933). Eliot's particular example, especially the establishment of an urban poetic world, fascinated Thomas in ways he had pointed to in a precocious schoolboy essay on 'Modern Poetry', written in 1929 at the age of fifteen for the *Swansea Grammar School Magazine*. And we cannot read later poems like 'In my craft or sullen art' (1945) or the villanelle to his father without thinking in both cases of Yeats. It is clear that Thomas was at all times imbued with admired voices, and no doubt the discovery of his own voice would have struck him as having little to do with the Swansea or the Wales he had inherited. In a series of essays on 'The Poets of Swansea', published in *The Herald of Wales* in 1932, especially in the tactful, critical politeness of those dealing with 'recent' poets like Howard Harris or James Chapman Woods, we detect the young man's longing to join, instead, a more modern poetic world. And that meant the 'English' poetic world. Certainly his correspondence with Pamela Hansford Johnson burns with the poet's conviction (as he felt it at the time at least) that, in Swansea, he was writing in a cultural vacuum.

This much has to be stated because the young Dylan's conscious concern was with contributing to the English poetic tradition, as tasted (if haphazardly) in the books which lined what he wittily called his father's 'brown study'. It is interesting, however, to come back at a view which suggests that a poet's immediate environment is nothing more than accidental: as if, as one critic quipped, Thomas's poems could have been written as well in Swanage as in Swansea. At the lowest level, we could counter quite easily. We could, for example, trace the phrase 'the ghost with a hammer, air' in 'If my head hurt a hair's foot' (1939) to a childhood which had once hero-worshipped the Welsh boxer Jimmy Wilde, nicknamed 'the ghost with a hammer in his hand'; or we could make a literary tour of Cwmdonkin Park, so often and literally celebrated in the poems. But the early Thomas is certainly not usually allusive in this objective, scenic way. The relevance of Swansea itself must therefore be sought on a deeper level. And yet in essence it is still an influence of quite conventional proportions: the effect of a society based largely on puritan and bourgeois values on a young sensibility reaching viable articulation in the middle of adolescent appetites and fears. Objectified into the 'subject' of a poem, this situation appears like the typical urge of youth towards some measure of moral freedom from conscience and etiquette:

> I have longed to move away
> From the hissing of the spent lie
> And the old terrors' continual cry
> Growing more terrible as the day
> Goes over the hill into the deep sea;
> I have longed to move away
> From the repetition of salutes,
> For there are ghosts in the air
> And ghostly echoes on paper,
> And the thunder of calls and notes.

In this objective form (the poem is 'I have longed to move away', first attempted in 1933) the poet can even see the opposite side of the coin: the poem's second stanza suggests that this world of 'Half convention and half lie' might prove a valuable corrective to morbid self-indulgence and personal uncertainties. But the point is that the situation is not often, like this, a poem's direct theme; it is more usually a complex of feelings resonant behind the poem's overt business.

Isolated in a social milieu he could not instinctively sanction, Thomas posed as visionary seer. The anti-poetic reality behind his pose was that of what in 'Do you not father me' (1935) he calls 'the wanton starer', the young adolescent casting a cold eye on life, on death. And indeed some of the poems have the mundane location of a view from the front window of No.5 Cwmdonkin Drive, overlooking the steep gradient of that suburban street, with Cwmdonkin Park across the road. But if the direct impulse of a poem came to him in the form of such a prospect, its emotions had a wider source. The puritan chapel-going culture of a place like Swansea was of course, in the thirties, already on the decline; but we must remember that the atmosphere surrounding our youth is that of our parents', not of our own, generation. Thomas would have been, under his father's free-thinking example, sufficiently dislodged from his environment to have some kind of perspective on it. Sunday school in his uncle David Rees's chapel, Paraclete, had certainly not yet grown into the beatific memory it was later to become in 'Poem in October' (1944)

> when he walked with his mother
> Through the parables
> Of sun light
> And the legends of the green chapels.

Instead, in April 1934, in a letter to Pamela Hansford Johnson, we find this gesture:

> Sunday in Wales. The Sunday-walkers have slunk out of the warrens in which they sleep and breed all the unholy week, have put on their black suits, reddest eyes, and meanest expressions, and are now marching up the hill past my window . . . I see the rehearsed gestures, the correct smiles, the grey cells revolving around nothing under the godly bowlers. I see the unborn children struggling up the hill in their mothers, beating on the jailing slab of the womb, little realizing what a smugger prison they wish to leap into.

And in 'I see the boys of summer' (1934), Thomas transforms this view of unborn children and frustrated youth into a symbolist indictment of their puritan nurture. The inhibiting attitudes of a restrictive adult culture are impeached in a dialectical pattern of images of fruition and decay. The 'frigid threads of doubt and dark' are the reality the young provincial sees behind the Victorian myth of love and light; and he seeks to demoralize the city fathers, whose voice he parodies in the line, 'O see the poles of promise in the boys' and which he sabotages with the irony of those phallic poles.

At an early stage, then, Thomas's literary weapon was a certain quality of sexual assertion, sharpened excitedly no doubt by that amount of puritanism which he did not himself escape. No doubt the sexual assertiveness bespoke a universal condition: one of Thomas's achievements was to make adolescence itself articulate. But, as in Lawrence's case, it also had something to do with a specific culture, in which Bible-based fears of Apocalypse enjoined retreat into social 'respectability'. It never drove Thomas, as it did Lawrence, to the exploration of a consistent compensating philosophy, but it certainly decided the emphasis of his protest in poems such as 'If I were tickled by the rub of love' or 'When, like a running grave' (1934):

> Joy is no knocking nation, sir and madam.

The 'Welshing rich' who 'play the proper gentleman and lady' in the poems are a kind of reluctant audience to the poet who saw himself as a 'dog among the fairies'. In this way, negatively, a society gave him a voice. Between the urgency of that voice in the early years and its more lyrical, later defence of Polly Garter against the gossip round the village pump came a levelling, compromising process. The gesture of protest remained the same, but softened. *Under Milk Wood* was a truce: the rebel ended off entertaining the enemy. The BBC has a way of refereeing these things.

Because I have tended to stress a social context, it should also be emphasized that its most general effect was to drive the young poet to explore its opposites. The overall phenomenon of the early poems, therefore, was the establishment of extra-social norms in the physical cotermination of man and nature, the discovery of cosmic parallels in the world of the human body, in poems such as 'Light breaks where no sun shines' or 'A process in the weather of the heart' (1934). The whole series of what have come by now to be called 'process' poems established elemental data deeper than social forms and etiquette.

A certain urgency also sprang from the poet's obscurity. The poems resist man's sometimes presumptuous knowingness about life. In league with the 'process' poems, where this resistance is tonally implied, is a series of poems like 'Why east wind chills'

(1933) and 'Should lanterns shine' (probably begun 1932, finished 1935), which poignantly assert the need for something like Keats's idea of 'Negative Capability' — a willingness to remain 'in uncertainties, Mysteries, doubts, without any irritable reaching after fact and reason'. The poignancy of the assertion is underlined and imaged in the poet's memories of an obscure childhood in school or park. As if to the manner born, there he was, turning intellectual vulnerability into virtue, learning to care and not to care, learning to sit still. In 'Why east wind chills' for example:

> I hear content, and 'Be content'
> Ring like a handbell through the corridors,
> And 'know no answer', and I know
> No answer to the children's cry
> Of echo's answer and the man of frost
> And ghostly comets over the raised fists,

or in 'Should lanterns shine':

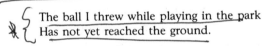

> The ball I threw while playing in the park
> Has not yet reached the ground.

Both the 'ghostly comets' and the 'ball I threw' — bred out of John Donne's image in the poem 'Go and catch a falling star' — are metaphors for the answers it is too early to receive and therefore too presumptuous to expect.

Cwmdonkin Park focused the confines of his world. Useful enough for urchin adventures, the park nevertheless also represented a pathetic suburban tendency to mime wilder forms of creative life. Indoors as well there was the dissatisfaction with potted fern and aspidistra, the fetishes of respectable poshness and tidiness. 'Especially when the October wind' (1934) warns the neighbours that the only context in which the young poet can accommodate them is that of organic life in which 'the wordy shapes of women' and 'the water's speeches' are merely coexistent data. The clock behind the pot of ferns, he says, will tell him less of Time than 'the signal grass which tells me all I know'. Paradoxically, this suburban round was such a vivid part of his memory that, writing to Vernon Watkins from Cornwall in April 1936, Thomas acknowledged its perhaps permanent grip on his personality:

I'd rather the bound slope of a suburban hill, the Elms, the Acacias, Rookery Nook, Curlew Avenue, to all these miles of green fields and flowery cliffs . . . I'm not a country man; I stand for, if anything, the aspidistra, the provincial drive.

But later, in 'After the funeral' (1938), as we shall see, he re-exercised his satiric spleen against such emblems. A satiric reflex was integral to his experience of the early years, and in this sense critics are wrong in arguing a greater 'honesty' for the prose over the poetry, simply on account of the prose's supposedly greater realism. Suburban complacency, indirectly targeted in the poems, was emotionally more stifling at the time than might be suggested by either the letter to Vernon Watkins or the comedy recollected in tranquillity of the *Portrait* stories.

Where *Portrait* stories such as 'The Peaches', 'A Visit to Grandpa's', 'Extraordinary Little Cough', or 'Who Do You Wish Was With Us?' are accurate is in their reworked memories of the compensating pull of pastoral. The countryside around and beyond Swansea was eternally present in the young Thomas's conscious-ness. But it is clear that he could not have written 'Fern Hill' or 'In the White Giant's Thigh' in, say, 1934. Nor could he have written his *Portrait of the Artist as a Young Dog* in the earlier years of the thirties, when he produced the surrealistic grotesqueries of stories such as 'The Burning Baby' or 'The Holy Six'. At that stage he was emotionally closer to Caradoc Evans than to Jack Jones or Gwyn Thomas.

London recognition and residence were to create, in the thirties, as easy a market for his short stories as for his poems. His reputation was given good initial impetus with poems in the *Adelphi*, the *Criterion* and *New Verse*, stories in the *New English Weekly*, *New Stories* and the *Adelphi*, and reviews in some of these and other reputable London periodicals. Thomas at this time took his short stories quite seriously, though he wrote them with considerably less effort and greater speed than his verse. Many of his best stories were first entered, between December 1933 and October 1934, in a 'Red Notebook' which, like the poetry ones, now rests in the Lockwood Memorial Library at Buffalo, New York. Off and on through the thirties he contemplated a novel of the Jarvis Valley, the mythic location of so many of the early tales. His conception of the novel as a juxtaposition of these individual stories is the first sign of his natural refusal to attempt larger, more demanding fictive structures in his work. This plan seemed suitable enough because the early stories were not in any way an examination of an objective world. In his correspondence with a Swansea friend, Trevor Hughes, he described such prose as the therapeutic expression of a sensibility, and their mawkish sexual emphasis as a mode of catharsis ('Everything I do drags up a devil'), which parallels his later, Freudian claim that his poetry brings hidden things into the nakedness of light. No doubt the grotesque pastoralism of these *pièces noires* stemmed from earlier vacation imaginings at Fernhill, with the spatial settings distorted. (It is obvious that the young boy who enjoyed Fernhill and the man who later remembered the boy were very different creatures and in a sense that difference provides the structure of the present essay.) The 'characters' of the early stories were Welsh conceptions — a dying poet, six vices personified as 'The Holy Six of Wales', a Reverend Davies, the notorious Dr Price of Llantrisant — but the ultimate subject was Thomas's own sensibility. The finest of the stories ('The Visitor', 'The Enemies', 'The Dress', for example) are impressive; but the overall manner was clearly and more importantly a phase in development. At their worst, they run to seed in two opposite directions: to either a self-conscious 'Anglo-Welsh' lyricism or a surrealistic exclusiveness which can seem too much an automatic slap in the reader's face.

We could illustrate this latter element startlingly from some of those stories (such as 'The School For Witches' or 'The Burning Baby') which at the time Thomas had to leave uncollected in the various periodicals of the thirties. A reputable publishing house like Dent, for whom the writer Richard Church acted as an intelligent but morally cautious Editor, and an association with whom was to the poet's ultimate good in saving him from a total reliance on more avant-garde publishers, finally accepted only the more restrained of the short stories. Seven of these were published, along with sixteen poems, in Thomas's third collection, *The Map of Love*, in 1939. But even these stories, which were accepted because their note of violence or arcane sexuality seemed relatively minimized, are essentially all of a piece with those others left out in the cold. They illustrate just as forcefully the young man's obsessive fusion of the objective reality of people, places and events (what Thomas calls 'the exterior world') with the distorted visions made out of them by the poet's deeper fears, the hysterical implosions of an imagination unable to accept order and control.

Whatever happened during those actual childhood holidays at Fernhill, it was remembered in the mid-thirties without that sense of a varied world and the reassuring light of common day which were to flood the poet's memory four years later in the *Portrait*, or ten years later in 'Fern Hill' itself. In the short story 'The Lemon' (1936), for example, it comes out like this:

> A storm came up, black boiled, from the sea, bringing rain and twelve winds to drive the hillbirds off the face of the sky; the storm, the black man, the whistler from the sea bottom and the fringe of the fish stones, the thunder, the lightning, the mighty pebbles, these came up; as a sickness, an afterbirth, coming up from the belly of weathers; mad as a mist coming up, the antichrist from a seaflame or a steam crucifix, coming up the putting on of rain; as the acid was stronger, the multiplying storm, the colour of temper, the whole, the unholy, rock-handed, came up coming up,
> This was the exterior world.
> And the shadows, that were web and cloven footed in the house, with the beaks of birds, the shifted shadows that bore a woman in each hand, had no casting substances; and the foam horses of the exterior sea climbed like foxes on the hills. This that held Nant and the doctor, the bone of a horse head, the ox and black manarising from the clay picture, was the interior world. This was the interior world where the acid grew stronger, and the death in the acid added ten days to the dead time.

The story, breaking like this without warnings from dream to reality, has a doctor figure who perpetrates vivisectionist outrages on ordinary forms of life; it opens with the doctor grafting a cat's head on to a chicken's trunk. The published example of Huxley's *Brave New World* (1932) might be relevant; but Thomas's natural resistance to cold forms of enquiry, scientific or otherwise, gives it a more autobiographical significance. Worth stressing here, however, is how much more controlled and persuasive an image of this 'irritable reaching after fact' is that which the poet had employed two years earlier in the poem 'Should lanterns shine', where man's insane quest for detachable knowledge is damned in a picture of the presumptuously premature opening of the grave's secrets:

Should lanterns shine, the holy face,
Caught in an octagon of unaccustomed light,
Would wither up, and any boy of love
Look twice before he fell from grace.
The features in their private dark
Are formed of flesh, but let the false day come
And from her lips the faded pigments fall,
The mummy cloths expose an ancient breast.

In the 'false day' of the lantern, the object of inquiry — the mummy's face — simply withers up. With this kind of intelligent economy, the more severe edges of Thomas's imagination are made to operate successfully, and in the service of insight and humane feeling. In comparison, the surrealism of the early short stories seems on the whole more indulgent and less profitable.

The surrealistic tendency in Thomas was natural — a means of concentrating on visionary rather than discursive talents — and it was sustained in his make-up in London as he became more fully aware of avant-garde periodicals such as *Contemporary Poetry and Prose*. In June 1936 he attended the International Surrealist Exhibition, carrying cups of boiled string and asking, 'Weak or strong?' Like his professed Communism, such gestures were no doubt fashionable parts of the act. But it would be silly to over-defend Thomas against certain surrealist implications in his poetry. It seems clear that the fashion and its possibilities gained quite a real hold on his imagination, reaching a climax in a prose piece such as 'In the Direction of the Beginning' (1938, printed in *A Prospect of the Sea*) or 'An Adventure from a Work in Progress' (published in *Seven*, Spring 1939); and in the images of poems such as the 'Altarwise by owl-light' sonnets (1935–6) or 'Because the pleasure-bird whistles' (1939). These works impress us more with the local outlandish image or phrase than with the satisfaction of a communicating whole. Their technique is defensible as the expression of manic tones of disenchantment, and Thomas seldom seems guilty of the mere automatic writing of the pure Surrealist. But such works are incapable of the wider range — the paradoxic fusion of innocence and experience, light and shade — which characterizes Thomas's best work, though of course such a judgement is only possible for us with the grace of hindsight. Thomas's career can be seen as a largely conscious movement towards the acceptance of a pre-lapsarian Edenic vision held in tension by a sense of paradox. In an early poem, as in the early stories, innocence and experience stood as disparate entities:

> We in our Eden knew the secret guardian
> In sacred waters that no frost could harden,
> And in the mighty mornings of the earth;
> Hell in a horn of sulphur and the cloven myth.

('Incarnate devil', 1933)

whereas 'Fern Hill' later fuses and balances the two notions in a phrase:

> Time held me green and dying,

where 'held' connotes *cradled* even while it insists on 'chained'.

To attend on the development of Thomas's career in this way is also to witness the reassembly of the human form. From the pre-natal imaginings of the early poems, to the dehumanized agent of 'The hand that signed the paper' (1933, Thomas's isolated concession to the political fashion of the thirties: compare Auden's 'The Tyrant'), to the embryonic bully of the birth scene in 'If my head hurt a hair's foot' (1939), to the 'war of burning brains and hair' of the wartime elegies of the early 1940s, the first half of his career shows the artist as if dissolving and fragmenting the human form in order to re-create its significance. The later poems, in contrast, celebrate a gallery of whole individuals: from his aunt Ann Jones in 'After the funeral' to the anonymous heroine of 'The tombstone told when she died' (1938), to 'The hunchback in the park' (1941), to the hunchback's pastoral extension in the form of the lonely man in 'A Winter's Tale' (1945), to the poet's son ('This side of the truth', 1945), to his daughter ('In Country Sleep', 1947), to himself in 'Fern Hill' (1945) remembered as 'prince of the apple towns', to the elegized milkmaids of 'In the White Giant's Thigh' (1950) or to his father too ready in his illness to go gentle into that good night in the famous villanelle. And one notices how often the dignity of the individual is redeemed, in the second half of the poet's career, by acts of memory and pastoral associations.

Indeed, a problem which increasingly faced Thomas in an acute form was exactly this one of the moral direction and development of his work, a development that was necessary if he was to expand and justify his early reputation. On the whole, I feel that the impasse (as he came to see it towards the end of the thirties) was momentarily broken by the new frame of mind which accompanied settlement in Laugharne in 1938, though this was inevitably punctuated (largely because of financial needs) by residence elsewhere, and especially by the pull of London which remained constant from his first move there in 1934. The deadlock itself was interesting. In one ironic sense it was caused by the straightforward conditions of his increasing reputation. When Thomas learned in April 1934 that his first volume of poems was a possibility, he quite rightly selected eighteen of his most recent efforts: thirteen poems came from the last of the four Notebooks, four from the period after the completion of the last Notebook, and 'Especially when the October wind' was radically revised from an earlier version for inclusion in *The Listener* two months before the appearance of *18 Poems* in December 1934. With such a remarkable and uncompromising collection under his belt, however, the inevitable follow-up of a second volume struck him as something more frightening than a challenge. For one thing, because of his highly crafted techniques, his production of new poems was painfully slow. For his second volume, *Twenty-five Poems* (September 1936), therefore, he had no option but to return to the Notebooks as his main source. The result was that some sixteen poems in *Twenty-five Poems* were revised versions of pre-1934 items from the Notebooks. On vacation in Donegal in the summer of 1935, and back in Swansea around Christmas, he methodically reactivated whole poems and parts of poems from his private early store. And it is not as if things changed with the third volume, either. *The Map Of Love* (August 1939) came after a period in which only five new poems had been achieved. Thus about half of the poety content of *The Map Of Love* was again of revised Notebook originals.

It could be claimed therefore that literary fame and expectation moved too quickly for Thomas's good. He did not, in the mid-thirties, while being much lionized in London, have time to explore in what ways a man of twenty-four might differ from a boy of nineteen. As stated, the root cause was the laboriousness of his chiselling craft. Even as early as May 1934 he had felt that all spontaneous impulse had faded: to Pamela Hansford Johnson he had written, 'the old fertile days are gone, and now a poem is the hardest and most thankless act of creation.' And looking back in a poem of 1938, he lamented that his art had been recently as if on the dole —

> On no work of words now for three lean months in the bloody
> Belly of the rich year and the big purse of my body
> I bitterly take to task my poverty and craft

('On no work of words') —

though, as with Wordsworth, Coleridge or Yeats, we do not believe a good poem when it tells us that good poetry is not possible. It may be significant that those lines just quoted were written after his move to Laugharne, where the more adult responsibilities of his own life first began to gather into perspective. He had married Caitlin Macnamara in July 1937, and at Laugharne they were awaiting the birth of their first child (Llewelyn, born January 1939).

From another angle, he saw the impasse unequivocally as a failure of humane commitment to recognizable human subjects. He saw that the difficulty sprang also from the very nature of his almost autonomous delight in language. And once again Thomas makes the critical accusation himself, in one of the finest of the shorter poems:

> Once it was the colour of saying
> Soaked my table the uglier side of a hill
> With a capsized field where a school sat still
> And a black and white patch of girls grew playing . . .
>
> Now my saying shall be my undoing,
> And every stone I wind off like a reel.

('Once it was the colour of saying')

In December 1938, when those lines were written, he sensed the real and dangerously aesthetic nature of his early poetic voice. Think of that word 'undoing' in the penultimate line: the implication is that his earlier poems had been not so much statements and explorations of experience as extensions of that experience into a kind of living fabric of words. John Bayley (in *The*

Romantic Survival, 1957) shrewdly pointed out that the essential characteristic of especially an early Thomas poem, and one he only intermittently avoided, was a resistance to what we might term a merely referential use of language. Instead of being *about* states of consciousness, a Thomas poem uses language as, in itself, a nervous, physical thing. It suggests an excitable way with words which we would more naturally associate with a writer whose first language was other than English. His compulsive punning, his listing in letters of favourite words at a remove (as we saw) from what they actually denote, or his persistence in claiming throughout his career that a good poet works 'out of words' and not 'towards' them: all this suggests a man happy (*à la* French Symbolists) to live in a world of words. Thus the following, unusually discursive, opening to a poem, suggesting a tremendous effort at avoiding his true voice —

> Out of the sighs a little comes,
> But not of grief, for I have knocked down that
> Before the agony; the spirit grows,
> Forgets, and cries;
> A little comes, is tasted and found good;
> All could not disappoint;
> There must, be praised, some certainty,
> If not of loving well, then not,
> And that is true after perpetual defeat
>
> ('Out of the sighs', 1934) —

cannot long avoid modulating into another, more nervous kind of poetry (see its second and third stanzas). As I say, 'Once it was the colour of saying' (1938) links this tendency — the tyranny of words, the autonomous colour of saying — to what Thomas took to be his inability to deal humanely with separate lives outside his own. What was at least in part a manifestation of the self-absorbed Welshness of his craft he took to be in another sense a failure of engagement with life.

Clearly, the ultimate sanction for the gradual development of a more 'public' voice had, in so sincere a poet, to come from within. But we can take the opportunity at this stage of also saluting the influence of Thomas's now famous correspondence with Vernon Watkins. This correspondence has a detailed bearing on Thomas's workmanlike concern with the craft of poetry, and covers the period from when Thomas was assembling the contents of *Twenty-five Poems* (1936) to the publication of *Deaths and Entrances* (1946). The correspondence, collected as *Letters to Vernon Watkins* (1957), speaks for itself on such questions as Thomas's wit, personal warmth, and poetic seriousness. But particularly fortunate in terms of personal reassurance was that Thomas should have found in Vernon Watkins, to whose noble generosity of spirit and critical intelligence he was only one witness, just the right kind of confidant. In the face of Thomas's often eccentric poetry, Watkins did not suffer from the kind of blank misgivings that afflicted Robert Bridges in relation to Hopkins or Thomas Wentworth Higginson *vis-à-vis* Emily Dickinson. This is not to say that Thomas and Watkins were technically kindred spirits. On the contrary, their correspondence is a wonderful way of gauging the radical differences between the two. Thomas frequently attacks Watkins's poems for their 'literary' deployment of language, when what Thomas wanted to see was what he called 'the strong, inevitable pulling that makes a poem an event, a happening, an action perhaps, not a still-life or an experience put down, placed, regulated'. And also instructive are the reasons he sometimes gives for not accepting some of Watkins's suggested alternatives for tentative phrases in Thomas's own poems (one suggested phrase Thomas considered 'esoterically off every mark in the poem'). What is clear, however, is that Watkins was both sympathetic to and convinced of the uniqueness of Thomas's genius. And basically reassured by that sympathy and conviction, Thomas was far more likely to reappraise his potential for development than if he had been faced by radical misgivings on Watkins's part. On one hand, therefore, Thomas was allowed his own convictions: two relative failures — the poems 'Now, Say nay' and 'How soon the servant sun' — went into *Twenty-five Poems* despite Watkins's submission that they 'presented a face of unwarrantable obscurity'. And on the other hand, with new poems, he showed himself more and more willing to be accountable to Watkins's better, but still unassuming, expectations. The autonomous privacy of the Notebooks was a thing of the past. The correspondence with Watkins was a further help for Thomas to see himself as he saw his friend — 'a person who has worked through all the beginnings and finds himself a new beginning in the middle'.

In terms of the poet's own imaginative autobiography, which is after all his recurrent mode, the difference between early and late is well illustrated if we juxtapose 'Where once the waters of your face' (1934) and 'Fern Hill' (1945). The earlier poem derives its imagery probably from a local Swansea feature, the tide which at times leaves the approach to the Worm's Head on the Gower Peninsula open and at other times cuts it off. (It was an area also described in his prose.) The poet uses the image of a free-flowing, abundant sea to suggest the optimism of his childhood self, the dry sea-bed symbolizing the poet's intimations of mortality which come with his growth to manhood. The connection with 'Fern Hill' is clear: both poems concern the loss of the visionary gleam and the celebration of the poet by his early world (compare 'spun to my screws' with the 'sang to my horn' in 'Fern Hill'). But the early poem, though by no means a crucially difficult one, does not, like 'Fern Hill', use sights, actions and sounds to confirm a shareable world. The affective quality of 'Where once the waters of your face' seems, in comparison to that masterpiece of memories about the Carmarthenshire farm, schematic and slight. One of the features worth keeping an eye on, therefore, is the measure of shareable emotion which the more leisurely narratives of the later poems enabled the poet to release. As I have stated, when Thomas the boy actually took those holidays at Fernhill he was a puzzled Swansea adolescent: when he later hoisted his memories into the present, he was a man shoring necessary delights against the ruins of an ugly war.

Before the outbreak of that war, Thomas had already begun to loosen the autonomous verbal structures of his verse and attempted what he would have regarded as the humanization of his craft. Marriage and approaching fatherhood helped constitute spheres of human relationship more clearly. But the density of his characteristic idiom could not suddenly change. The cool objectivity of those poems (poems such as 'Once it was the colour of saying') in which he talks *about* the problem was one thing: returning to less self-conscious themes was another. A further point worth recording is that Thomas's naturally expansive manner seems ill-suited to those themes which are irretrievably personal or domestic, like love-anger or jealousy. Poems stemming from his relationship with his wife Caitlin — poems such as 'Not from this anger', 'I make this in a warring absence' (both 1938) and 'Into her lying down head' (1940) — show a critical disproportion between their manner and their matter. The Welsh element in Thomas — what has been loosely, though not wrongly, called the 'Bardic' element (the tradition of 'praise poetry', of 'speaking for the race') — was not geared to the exploration of utterly individual or domestic emotion. That 'Bardic' element depends, rather, on the poet's ability to engage his emotions on wider, more representative, levels. At its lowest level, this voice, still heard in areas of Welsh Wales, is a mere unembarrassed readiness to celebrate persons, events or geography in a kind of blanketing occasional manner. So we must add one other condition to our definition of Thomas's 'Bardic' quality: that the 'representative', collective element should be sharpened by just the right measure of personal engagement on his part. 'Speaking for the race' can be an arid exercise if we do not sense at the same time that the speaker has a local habitation and a name. We are about to see this judicious balance in one of Thomas's finest poems, 'After the funeral (In memory of Ann Jones)'. In preparation, we might mention first a little-known poem of the same period, 'The tombstone told when she died'. Coming to it from the poems to Caitlin, poems whose art can appear too much a case of killing one bird with three stones, what we notice is the dilution in the poem's manner. Resurrected from an unsatisfactory fragment in the February 1933 Notebook, it has the old pre-natal perspective of the early poems still functioning, but we feel that this is now being regulated in a more dramatically affective way:

> I who saw in a hurried film
> Death and this mad heroine
> Meet once on a mortal wall
> Heard her speak through the chipped beak
> Of the stone bird guarding her:
> I died before bedtime came
> But my womb was bellowing
> And I felt with my bare fall
> A blazing red harsh head tear up
> And the dear floods of his hair.

> ('The tombstone told when she died', 1938)

The real test had come a few months previously when Thomas had forced a confrontation with his emotional responsiveness in

33

terms of a less anonymous elegy — that on the death of Annie Jones, the kindly aunt who had presided over his countless schoolboy holidays at Fernhill. In the February 1933 Notebook version of 'After the funeral' he had exercised nothing but the satiric spleen which, as we have seen, marked so much of his reaction to Welsh experience in those early years. And indeed, while his aunt actually lay dying in a Carmarthen hospital in 1933, his reaction (recorded in a letter of January 1933 to Trevor Hughes) had been one of hopeless disaffection:

> But the foul thing is I feel utterly unmoved, apart, as I said, from the pleasant death-reek at my negroid nostrils. I haven't really the faintest interest in her or her womb. She is dying. She is dead. She is alive. It is all the same thing. I shall miss her bi-annual postal orders. And yet I like — liked her. She loves — loved — me. Am I, he said with the diarist's unctuous, egotistic preoccupation with his own blasted psychological reactions to his own trivial affairs, callous and nasty? Should I weep? Should I pity the old thing? For a moment I feel I should. There must be something lacking in me. I don't feel worried, or hardly ever, about other people. It's self, self, all the time. I'm rarely interested in other people's emotions, except those of my pasteboard characters. I prefer (this is one of the thousand contradictory devils speaking) style to life, my own reactions to emotions rather than the emotions themselves. Is this, he pondered, a lack of soul?

In the spring of 1938 he had to make a fresh attempt at the elegy, and to make amends. It is therefore probably no mere accident that sandwiched the 1938 version of 'After the funeral' between two other treatments of the insensitive tyranny of words ('The spire cranes' and 'Once it was the colour of saying') in the arrangement of *The Map of Love* volume in 1939. In that totally rewritten version of 'After the funeral' Thomas highlights the most pressing problem ever to worry him in the implications of his verbally energetic craft. To what degree can language be genuinely creative? Can it mime the miracle of resurrection? The query is present in the way in which the poem's language insists on its own, cold and lapidary quality: 'for this *memorial*'s sake' . . . 'this skyward *statue*' . . . 'Is *carved* from her' . . . And *sculptured* Ann is seventy years of *stone*' . . . 'this *monumental* argument of the *hewn* voice'. The challenge on which the poem is built is that of rising above this recognized deficiency, to shout affirmation in the face of coldly realized odds. But the revised version, with a necessary honesty, also states the danger of being verbally overblown, of being 'blindly magnified out of praise'. It also did well to retain some of the satiric, disaffected vision of the poet's younger self, as it had manifested itself in the first version in 1933 and in that painful letter to Trevor Hughes. Thus in the very opening lines the mourners are seen with the grotesque eye of the satirical 'wanton starer' that Thomas had once been:

> After the funeral, mule praises, brays,
> Windshake of sailshaped ears, muffle-toed tap
> Tap happily of one peg in the thick
> Grave's foot, blinds down the lids, the teeth in black,
> The spittled eyes, the salt ponds in the sleeves . . .

The continuation into the new poem of the old callousness, of the old suspicion of social hypocrisy, shows how he was grappling as much with an idea of himself as with the memory of Ann Jones. By exercising he was also exorcising the old disenchantment.

Another stroke of genius was to pivot the poem's affirmation on those emblems of the Welsh parlour, the stuffed fox and the potted fern. This seems true to a particularly Welsh experience — as anyone will realize who has, as a child, found himself in the cold silence of best rooms on funeral days, or ever felt tempted to poke sweet-papers into the mouths of the foxes' heads once worn by praying matrons in chapel. The poem is true to a Welsh atmosphere which has only disappeared from custom and ceremony in the last generation or so. It is because it is balanced against this communal atrophy that the threatening deadlock in the poet's own craft and sullen art is communicated with a sense of tension. Against these petrifying odds, the imaginative release (and we can only expect it to be an *imaginative* release) of the final affirmative flourish does more to honour Ann Jones than any sentimental memories would have accomplished:

> Storm me for ever over her grave until
> The stuffed lung of the fox twitch and cry Love
> And the strutting fern lay seeds on the black sill.

This is an imagistic stroke worthy of comparison with Yeats's symbolist deployment of the chestnut tree and the dance at the end of 'Among School Children'. And its magnanimity is significantly heightened, it seems to me, by the fact that Thomas remembers Ann Jones as being so concretely a part of a Welsh puritan ethos from which he had earlier turned away in mere recoil:

> I know her scrubbed and sour humble hands
> Lie with religion in their cramp. . .

In 1938 Dylan Thomas was in this way in a position to enter more and more into an exploration of, and a relationship with, the Welshness of his roots. In 'After the funeral', Wales and Welsh life, and more importantly their hold on the poet's sensibility, had come to the surface with certain pressures on his objective acceptance of his cultural heritage. Looking back down the line of poems written up to this time, we find no real equivalent to this grappling with the roots of his own consciousness. Tied in with the experience of 'After the funeral' is a recognition of the wilder inheritance that lay behind the suburban tidiness of his parents' home, that home which during the thirties bounced him back to London by a process of natural recoil. Thomas is a curious case within these shores, and in our own time, of cultural dispossession. Before 1938, he had always been able to spin the 'Bardic' magic of incidental phrases like 'the loud hill of Wales' or 'Under the lank, fourth folly on Glamorgan's hill'; and to the end of his life his public image demanded jokey responses like 'Land of my fathers, my fathers can keep it'. But 'After the funeral' in 1938 was an act of pure attention.

The chance to follow through, and diversify, this kind of achievement was denied the poet at a time when it seemed most promising. As stated, it was in 1938 that Thomas moved to Laugharne, and that was also the year in which he started the short stories of his *Portrait*. Laugharne was of course a town with completely its own (and in many ways non-Welsh) character. But its proximity to Fernhill country was significant. The isolated eccentricities of 'this timeless, beautiful, barmy (both spellings) town', as Thomas was to describe it in one of his last radio broadcasts, satisfied his constant need for local, uncompromising colour while at the same time providing him with a background redolent of memories attaching to Fernhill and to nearby family cottages at Blaen Cwm, where the teenager had often stayed and written poetry. The *Portrait* story called 'The Peaches' (contemporary, we must remember, with 'After the funeral') illustrates the attention to detail and atmosphere which suggests a man getting to grips with the sights and smells of his mundane inheritance:

> The best room smelt of moth balls and fur and damp and dead plants and stale, sour air. Two glass cases on wooden coffin-boxes lined the window sill. You looked at the weed-grown vegetable garden through a stuffed fox's legs, over a partridge's head, along the red-paint-stained breast of a stiff wild duck. A case of china and pewter, trinkets, teeth, family brooches, stood beyond the bandy table; there was a large oil lamp on the patchwork table-cloth, a Bible with a clasp, a tall vase with a draped woman about to bathe on it, and a framed photograph of Annie, Uncle Jim, and Gwilym smiling in front of a fern-pot.

Capitalization on memory and nostalgia has often been criticized in Thomas's work. But it might be suggested that such involvement with the past was symptomatic at this stage of an increasing rootedness in the present. It is no accident that the idea which was, in ten years' time, to become *Under Milk Wood* first occurred to the poet round about this period. To some degree he was reinheriting his own people; a long-necessary anchorage in a particular locale seemed possible. London in itself had already begun to pall — but with the added complication of its continuing seductiveness and, as war approached, the realization that without it there would be no daily bread. I think that in two poems of 1939 Thomas recognized how fragile his anchorage was. Remembering Wilfred Owen's 'The Promisers' ('When I awoke, the glancing day looked gay'), he started a poem, 'When I woke, the town spoke' and lamented that Laugharne, his 'sea town was breaking'; and in 'Once below a time', laughing at his 'young dog' and London self, he yearned for what, in December 1939, must have seemed impossible:

> mostly bare I would lie down,
> Lie down, lie down and live
> As quiet as a bone.

In three months' time he was writing 'The Countryman's Return' (published in *The Cambridge Front*, Summer 1940), a poem in which, in the conditions of London life and war, the disinheritance of his pastoral roots has become a superficial joke in doggerel.

Another way in which we might register the same point would be by juxtaposing *Adventures in the Skin Trade* with the *Portrait* stories. Whatever comic appeal the former work (written mid-1941) may have, it seems clear that it was in the first place something far more trivial (the word is Thomas's own) than the memories activated in the *Portrait*. The unfinished novel is the half-imagined story of the young Dylan's first initiation into London life as it had occurred some eight or nine years previously. Chronologically, therefore, its biography was meant to carry on from where the *Portrait* stories had left off. In one particular way it was a trivialization of what in the actual poet was a central strength, what we have called the stance of Negative Capability. Vernon Watkins recalled Thomas's overall plan for the novel: 'The central character . . . would attract adventures to him by his own unadventurous stillness and natural acceptance of every situation.' The first publishers to whom it was submitted rejected it, and Thomas's own view of the work was in reality not far from theirs: 'It's the only really dashed-off piece of work I remember doing.' The first effect of the war on Thomas's career was to force into prominence the most obviously 'professional' aspects of his art, the pot-boiling talents. The ear for dialogue displayed in *Adventures in the Skin Trade* is not negligible, but the general effect is too often second-hand. Thomas himself acknowledged Dickens, Kafka and Beachcomber, and we would be paying him too much of a compliment to think those mixed references only a joke.

The professionalism in itself, of course, is beyond attack, and the film-scripts which he wrote during the war years are in many ways admirable examples of work done in a most demanding medium. The finest of them, *The Doctor and the Devils* (finished October 1944), about the exploits of Burke and Hare, the nineteenth-century Edinburgh body-snatchers, exhibits an assured sense of atmospheric drama as well as decisive skills in characterization. Even in its incidentals we are aware of those sharp verbal touches which confirm our impression of a very intelligent writer ('There are many, many children, some very old'). Again, in his film-script of the first half of Maurice O'Sullivan's *Twenty Years A-Growing* (1944), Thomas matched with admirable care the lyrical poignancy of that classic autobiography of a childhood spent on the Blasket Islands, off Kerry:

> Through this we see a LONG SHOT of Maurice and Mickil walking in a meadow, picking flowers. Half the great meadow is in sunlight. Half in deep dusk through which we see the strange shapes of trees moving and strange hills.
>
> Closer now, we see the children sit down by a stream, their arms full of flowers. They sit in the sunlight. We hear birds singing above them, but, from a distance, we hear, too, the note of the owl as though it came from the dark half of the great meadow.

But there was another poignancy there. The man who wrote those words was the man who in 1939 had had to abandon 'Poem in October', a poem of which the above lines are bound to remind us. Visionary memories of childhood which a pre-war quietus in Laugharne must have prompted had proved, in the actual event of war, impossible; but, as we shall see, four years of war were to make them in the end irresistibly necessary.

Thomas's reaction to the onset of war strikes us at first as, comically, one of panic. In his letters he started to scrabble and scratch for assurances of personal safety and domestic survival. Inscribing a copy of the newly published *The Map of Love* for Pamela Hansford Johnson on 3 September 1939, he added under the date, 'Dylan-shooting begins'. He started eagerly to enquire about the possibility of getting one of the 'reserved occupations' in the Ministry of Information or the BBC, or about the requirements for conscientious objection. He even asked whether membership of the Welsh Nationalist Party might secure exemption. The permutations of protest in the letters ranged from dramatic cowardice ('My little body I don't intend to waste'), to an obsession with time ('all I want is time to write poems'), to an attempt at philosophic refusal in the form of a young writers' manifesto, to plangent disappointment:

> It is terrible to have built, out of nothing, a complete happiness — from no money, no possessions, no material hopes — and a way of living, and then to see the immediate possibility of its being exploded and ruined through no fault of one's own.
>
> (Letter to his father, August 1939)

Expressed differently to suit different correspondents, these were all sincere reactions in confusion. But behind the gestures of panicked self-regard lay a deeper reaction, and one more relevant to his art:

profound moral shock. Thomas's personal survival during the war was in the event assured by various means. A C3 medical rating (weak lungs) depressed him but kept him safe; friends, literary and other, organized financial support; script-writing for the Latin American Service of the BBC was followed by what was to prove his financial mainstay — work on documentary film-scripts for Strand Films under the monopolizing aegis of the Ministry of Information; and later in the war came the famous BBC broadcasts. These accidental rescues took care of themselves. But they did not dispel the feeling of moral insult which became strong in Thomas from the first London air-raids onwards. The deeper levels of his emotional life could not be paraded in cold prose. The clowning of the correspondent and man-about-London were strategies for survival. Only the wartime poems themselves could intimate the man's deepest reactions.

Poems such as 'There was a saviour', 'Deaths and Entrances', 'Among those Killed in the Dawn Raid was a Man Aged a Hundred', 'Ceremony after a Fire Raid' and 'A Refusal to Mourn the Death, by Fire, of a Child in London' characterize the shock. A new area of experience became demandingly real. And with an ironic, if unconscious, gesture, Thomas in 1941 sold his Notebooks to America, via a 'House of Books' sale catalogue, the four poetry Notebooks reaping for the now penniless poet a mere £25. In selling the Notebooks, he marked the point of no return. Constantine FitzGibbon notes the irony: Thomas was at the age at which Keats had died.

An interesting aspect of the wartime elegies, coming to them chronologically from, say, 'After the funeral', 'A saint about to fall' or 'Once it was the colour of saying', is the way in which they function with the minimum sense of authorial (as opposed to wartime) context. Their occasional nature — responding to deaths in the bombing raids on London — emphasizes a quality of bardic impersonality, even while highlighting once and for all the doctrinal limits of Thomas's religious view of life. The shift of attention and energy to London, when two years previously they had looked as if they might have centred at Laugharne, found Thomas without a background. The result is that the poems bring out in curiously clear form some of the essential properties of Thomas's poetic voice. We might list these as follows: a dependence on *affirmation* as opposed to any other kind of emotional or intellectual persuasiveness (contrast that abandoned relic of early Auden, '1st September 1939'); an uncanny inter-penetration of things, emotions, and events by a kind of metaphysical *awareness* which seems in any case to predate the poem's actual data; a strong impression of the poem as *something accomplished*, an achieved form, beyond assent or disagreement. In talking about a poem like 'There was a saviour' (1940), therefore, our possible mistrust of its intellectual authority on its theme (the Church's perversion of Christ's original teaching into a closed, desensitized system) fades in our sense of the poem's urgency:

> When hindering man hurt
> Man, animal, or bird
> We hid our fears in that murdering breath,
> Silence, silence to do, when earth grew loud,
> In lairs and asylums of the tremendous shout.

Likewise with 'A Refusal to Mourn' (1945). Only away from the poem do we ask what kind of presumption it takes to achieve these assertive cadences in the act of *refusing* to mourn:

> Deep with the first dead lies London's daughter,
> Robed in the long friends,
> The grains beyond age, the dark veins of her mother,
> Secret by the unmourning water
> Of the riding Thames.
> After the first death, there is no other.

But a hostile critic might ask that kind of question more often. One kind of answer would draw an analogy between Thomas's art and other vocal traditions which we think of as having particularly Welsh versions: the kind of sermon or political speech which relies less on theology or logic than on an accumulative, tonal persuasiveness. It is not so much a question of how many examples of pulpit or platform *hwyl* Thomas himself may have witnessed, as what makes the phenomenon in the first place characteristically Welsh. There can be no doubt that in Wales, as in regions of England, it has historically had a lot to do with the character of little-educated, depressed communities, and that the continuation of the element of zeal was assured for the Wales of our time by the *diwygiadau* or religious revivals of the early years of the twentieth century. Its historical character is of course a subject for individual attention. What seems relevant here is that Thomas's manner is instinctively imbued by his unacknowledged fathers' ghosts and voices. Clark Emery, in *The World of Dylan Thomas* (1962), suggests that the whole point of 'Among those Killed in the Dawn Raid' (1941) is an ironic one: the futile, technological slaughter of a centenarian! The irony is certainly there in Thomas's use of an actual newspaper heading as title; but our overall experience of the poem itself suggests something less sharp, less individual. The poem's procedure, like that of 'A Refusal to Mourn', is more clearly the absorbed rhetoric of a pulpit or graveside occasion, minus only a doctrinal quality in its offered comfort:

> The morning is flying on the wings of his age
> And a hundred storks perch on the sun's right hand.

This group of war elegies gets to look increasingly impressive as the years go by. The delayed quality of their appeal is even appropriate. Keith Douglas once said that the full body of Second World War poetry would not be completed till after the war was over. In the same way, the very variety of what we mean by that war poetry has only subsequently become visible. Yeats (died 1939), with his sensing of a 'blood dimmed tide', is part of the picture; experiences or truths as seen by non-combatants like Thomas weigh in with those of the combatants; poems not strictly *about* the war (Eliot's *Four Quartets*) share authority with those more directly prompted by it. And it is only at this remove that the exact strength of Thomas's elegies is visible. They are the most positive of the poems produced by that war, affirming life and sexuality, refusing to mourn, evoking entrances as well as deaths, offering ceremonies after fire-raids. In a curious way, all this is closer to the real temper of the time — to the resilience and the guts — than the poems of poets who travelled towards the war along more purely ideological routes.

Between 1941 and 1944 Thomas wrote hardly any new poems. His wife felt sure that the corruption of London life and what she saw as his irrelevant work in films were halting the poet's real development. She was, incidentally, to continue this role of involved and intelligent wardenship of Thomas's better interests.

No doubt, the relative poetic silence of the 1941–4 period was indeed due mainly to mundane inconvenience. But the unsettledness was also more profound. Thomas seemed happiest during these years when he was back in Wales — in Swansea, Laugharne, Talsarn or New Quay. Wartime London must have struck him with the overpowering sense of fragmentary present-tense experience. Wales on the other hand always kept him in touch with the past — largely his own, but also with a feeling of wider rootedness. The function of elegiac memory was to prove the best line of development out of the lean years. It can, for example, be no accident that the only poem he chose to rework from the early Notebooks after he had sold them was 'The hunchback in the park', whose resurrection occurred, paradoxically, in the same month (July 1941) as the writing of 'Among those Killed in the Dawn Raid'. In contrast with the latter poem, the experience of the 'Hunchback' poem, relayed from out of the Swansea past, prompted the poet to reassemble, momentarily, his sense of place and geography in relation to his own spiritual development.

But of course what Wales really provided when the war years seemed endless was that pastoral context which generated also the most expansive store of imagery and sensation for the final stage of the poet's career. Much of the poignancy of the London war elegies stems from our sense of a curiously frustrated pastoralism, deployed in the face of shock and disgust:

> Secret by the unmourning water
> Of the riding Thames.

And it was this element, released, which flooded back into the poet's voice when, in 1944, he returned to complete 'Poem in October', describing it to Vernon Watkins, significantly, as a 'Laugharne poem: the first place poem I've written':

> It turned away from the blithe country
> And down the other air and the blue altered sky
> Streamed again a wonder of summer
> With apples
> Pears and red currants
> And I saw in the turning so clearly a child's
> Forgotten mornings when he walked with his mother
> Through the parables
> Of sun light
> And the legends of the green chapels.

Again, what seems peculiarly Welsh about this luminous poem is the way in which its structure is provided not by argumentative development, but by the tonal unity of its geographic narrative. This is what relates it, on a level deeper than ordinary literary influence, to, let us say, Henry Vaughan's 'Regeneration':

> Here, I repos'd; but scarse well set,
>   A grove descryed
> Of stately height, whose branches met
>   And mixt on every side;
> I entred, and once in
>   (Amaz'd to see't),
> Found all was chang'd, and a new spring
>   Did all my senses greet;
>
> The unthrift Sunne shot vitall gold
>   A thousand peeces,
> And heaven its azure did unfold
>   Checqur'd with snowie fleeces,
> The aire was all in spice
>   And every bush
> A garland wore; Thus fed my Eyes
>   But all the Eare lay hush.

Thomas, in a broadcast on 'Welsh Poets' (1946), spoke of Vaughan's 'authentic and intense vision' moving across 'a wild, and yet inevitably ordered, sacred landscape'.

As if in reaction to a process of stultification, memories of childhood had already started to become a species of spontaneous therapy. In February 1943 Thomas had broadcast his 'Reminiscences of Childhood' on the BBC — a medium which provided him with supplementary support from 1937 to the end of his life. *Deaths and Entrances*, Thomas's fourth volume of poetry (February 1946), illustrates quite equally the polarity between released lyricism ('Poem in October' and 'Fern Hill') and shocked assertion ('Deaths and Entrances' and 'Ceremony after a Fire Raid') which epitomized his wartime existence. Both types were in their own way responses to an emergency. But if one were prompted to evaluation, it seems reasonably clear that the outstanding achievement in *Deaths and Entrances* is 'Fern Hill'. And one of its central implications is the defeat of cynicism. Like the tone and childhood images of Eliot's later verse, a poem like 'Fern Hill' illustrates finally the movement of Thomas's career towards warm assertion. The context out of which it sprang was the strange resurgence of creativity which came to him in the last two years of the war, based in Llan-gain (with Laugharne still in view) and in New Quay. We must link to this new lease of energy the fact that *Under Milk Wood* was also started at the same time.

It will have been clear already, in asides, that parts of this essay have been modulated with the hindsight which a fine poem like 'Fern Hill' necessarily provides. There we were aimed. It seems suitable that the published volume which finally established Thomas's reputation as an important poet should have included such an intelligently unembarrassed orchestration. The surrenders which had been made to a fashionable and natural surrealism in the thirties, and the anarchic levels of narrative which had clotted and distanced an autobiography like the 'Altarwise' sonnet sequence some ten years before, were no longer a threat or a necessity. In the earlier idiom, the only alternative stylistic mode for self-elegy had seemed to be the uncharacteristically bald economy of poems such as 'Should lanterns shine' (1934) or 'Twenty-four years' (1938). And this helps us make our first point about 'Fern Hill': that, with a new kind of narrative discipline, it validated the natural expansiveness of Thomas's more characteristic poetic voice.

The most common charge against 'Fern Hill' has been that of an escapist, bourgeois indulgence, an insult given some comparative edge in Roy Fuller's jibe, 'dilute Wordsworthianism'. As a set of pastoral memories, 'Fern Hill' has given a younger generation of poets and critics something either to respect or to react against. Even a poet like Philip Larkin (himself superbly capable of Hardy-like plangencies, and an admirer of Thomas) must have had Thomas partly in mind in the witty non-elegy called 'I remember, I remember':

> And here we have that splendid family
>
> I never ran to when I got depressed,
> The boys all biceps and the girls all chest,
> Their comic Ford, their farm where I could be
> 'Really myself'. I'll show you, come to that,
> The bracken where I never trembling sat . . .

But any notion that 'Fern Hill' is simply Thomas Hood's

'I remember, I remember the house where I was born . . .' writ large ignores the intelligence of its detailed organization, and especially the way in which its accumulative movement is justified by the functional richness of its associations at every stage. Close reading confirms a sense, not of diffuseness, but of economy. It will be useful, and a pleasure, to have a reminder of its texture in front of us:

> Now as I was young and easy under the apple boughs
> About the lilting house and happy as the grass was green,
> > The night above the dingle starry,
> > > Time let me hail and climb
> > Golden in the heydays of his eyes,
> And honoured among wagons I was prince of the apple towns
> And once below a time I lordly had the trees and leaves
> > > Trail with daisies and barley
> > Down the rivers of the windfall light.
>
> And as I was green and carefree, famous among the barns
> About the happy yard and singing as the farm was home,
> > In the sun that is young once only,
> > > Time let me play and be
> > Golden in the mercy of his means,
> And green and golden I was huntsman and herdsman, the calves
> Sang to my horn, the foxes on the hills barked clear and cold,
> > > And the sabbath rang slowly
> > In the pebbles of the holy streams.
>
> All the sun long it was running, it was lovely, the hay
> Fields high as the house, the tunes from the chimneys, it was air
> > And playing, lovely and watery
> > > And fire green as grass . . .

The style has a quicksilver effect of releasing secondary 'ghost' effects simultaneously with its primary statements. The result is a liquid movement which demands the reader's attention on various levels at once. Thus in stanza one, both the boy *and* the apple boughs are syntactically 'About the lilting house'. Similarly, 'Time let me hail and climb' is simultaneously abstract assertion and concrete description of the child stopping and climbing onto the apple carts. 'Golden in the heydays of his eyes' refurbishes the cliché whereby one thinks oneself the apple of somebody's eye; and in the context 'heydays' registers also as *hay-days*. 'Once below a time', at first a facile pun, draws its poignancy from the innocent presumption of that 'climb' we encountered three lines back; the child is indeed 'below' (subject to) time, especially with night 'above'. The 'windfall light' suggests, all at once, beams of dappled sunlight through shuttering branches, or again literally the light on early-fallen apples, or an abstract idea of premature enlightenment. In stanza two, again, both the boy *and* the barns are 'About the happy yard'. And 'Singing as the farm was home' suggests *because the farm was home* and (by analogy with 'happy as the grass was green') that the boy was singing *as surely as the farm was home*. Again, in the lines

> Time let me play and be
> Golden in the mercy of his means

Time let the boy play; Time let him exist; Time let him play and let him alone; and Time let him play and be golden: all because of the way Thomas has split the sentence over the line-break. Most of those meanings would disappear if the two lines were written out as one.

In stanza three, the phrase 'rang slowly' from the previous stanza has suggested (through the association of 'streams') an analogous ghost phrase, *ran slowly;* so that stanza three opens, 'All the sun long it was running' — with a sense of connection between stanzas which we feel but cannot point to. And that 'rang' at the end of the second stanza has brought another sequence of images to the threshold of stanza three: the musical associations of 'lilting', 'singing', 'play', 'sang' and 'rang' continue into the third stanza without detriment to the literal business of 'tunes', 'air' and 'playing'. It is this sequence which gives the poem's final line,

> Though I sang in my chains like the sea,

an echoing base in the poem's musical imagery, and saves it from isolated sentiment. Stanza three also makes us unsuspecting witnesses to the four elements of creation, making them dance into life:

> it was air
> And playing, lovely and watery
> And fire green as grass.

If 'fire green as grass' puzzles us for a moment, a phrase from stanza one ('happy as the grass was green') helps us take it as meaning *fire as intensely red as grass is green*.

And so on — to the embarrassment only of someone other than the poet and his poem or an alert reader. What is called for is not an adjudication on the cleverness or otherwise of any one of these examples, but an openness to their overall aim of reconstituting in us the simultaneity of the child's responses. John Malcolm Brinnin records that he saw at the Boat House in Laugharne (where he had come to persuade Thomas to visit America) over two hundred worksheets for 'Fern Hill'. The reader's business is to test whether such energy lives also on the page. The poem's achievement lies in remaining faithful to two psychologies at once: that of the child and that of the grown man, that of innocence and that of experience. It does not merely denote the boy's rapture: it enacts it. The accumulative framework of the poem's thirty-two 'ands' resurrects the child's hectic voice as an experience, something more than a mere notion. In the final stanza, the only one in which adult reflection is in complete control, 'and' has become a tamer link-word *inside* the sentence, whereas throughout the first five stanzas it has also been, ironically, a strenuous avoidance of the full stop. After all, three stanzas actually *start* with 'And'. The child's voice is also caught in that relaxed and dangerously repeated 'lovely' in stanza three: 'lovely' is the one word a child uses more meaningfully than an adult. With another example ('nice'), a section from the short story 'A Prospect of the Sea' explains the force of that repeated word 'lovely':

> He could think of no words to say how wonderful the summer was, or the noise of the wood-pigeons, or the lazy corn blowing in the half wind from the sea at the river's end. There were no words for the sky and the sun and the summer country: the birds were nice, and the corn was nice.

Through an attention to pace and texture, Thomas seems able to rival in words visionary effects more often associated with other, more visual, media: we see this if we think of 'Poem in October' and, say, Monet's painting *The Poppy Field*, or if we compare 'Fern Hill' with Chagall's technique of causing images to float in lilting spatial relationship the one with the other. But its greatness is still that inward connectiveness of its language. C. Day Lewis once wrote a parody of 'Fern Hill''s manner (in *An Italian Visit*, 1953), proving only one thing: that an assemblage of 'Fern Hill''s incidentals is no automatic reproduction of its resonant toughness.

'Fern Hill' and 'Poem in October' assert the kind of child's innocence which at the time is only possible in the absence of reflection, like the unselfconsciousness of the boy in the *Portrait* story 'Extraordinary Little Cough', whose events took place, Thomas wrote, 'some years before I knew I was happy'. In other words, the very condition of such events is a version of Negative Capability, seen as a kind of Edenic instinctiveness. 'Fern Hill', especially, has also an assertive quality ('Oh as I was . . .') bred in reaction to the atmosphere which prevailed at the end of the war, when immediate victory seemed dirtied by the irreversible implications of Hiroshima and Nagasaki, and by the kind of news which now filtered through about Nazi atrocities and the concentration camps. After such knowledge, what forgiveness? Thomas later lamented the implications for 'this apparently hell-bent world' in the plan he outlined for his long series of projected poems to be called collectively 'In Country Heaven', of which the three late poems 'In Country Sleep', 'Over Sir John's hill' and 'In the White Giant's Thigh' were simply meant to be a part. 'The earth', he said in a 1950 broadcast, 'has killed itself. It is black, petrified, wizened, poisoned, burst; insanity has blown it rotten.'

No doubt, on a more personal level, he felt the encroachment also of middle age and its responsibilities: a second child, Aeronwy, had been born in 1943. Nothing serves more than the increase of a family to give that sense of something pushing one to the edge of one's own life. This must have been especially so in the face of the poet's father's increasing infirmity. Thomas's relationship with his father over the years of his growing fame had moreover developed into something more orthodoxly affectionate. Our beginnings never know our ends. It was probably in the same year as 'Fern Hill' (1945) that he also started 'Do not go gentle into that good night', though it was not finished till about 1951. It is worth making the point that, in contrast with the more loosely confessional 'Elegy' on his father which Thomas left unfinished at his own death, his best effects were still gained when difficult emotion had to animate a fettering technical form such as the villanelle, the possibilities of which he had probably grasped in the superb example of William Empson's poetry. As John Donne put it, 'Grief brought to numbers cannot be so fierce/For, he tames it that fetters it in verse.'

From the end of the war to 1949 the poet lived mainly in London and Oxford, with visits to Ireland, Italy and Prague (as a guest of the Czechoslovak government). One idea already in his mind at the end of the war was of emigration to America. The same hectic opportunism which had characterized his reaction to the outbreak of war marks his letters on this possibility to English and American friends. His reputation in the States was already being felt — he was, for one thing, in 1945 awarded the Levinson Poetry Prize of the *Poetry* (Chicago) magazine — and his plans for emigration were, as far as he was concerned, urgent. Edith Sitwell, who had early (though not always intelligently) heralded his genius, he now saw as a guarantor of lecturing and reading engagements in America, an arrangement which in the event became the pattern from 1950 onwards, but under the organization (and, as it turned out, the observant eye) of John Malcolm Brinnin. But initially the plan, with Caitlin's agreement, had been for definite emigration, and Thomas had seriously considered a job with *Time* magazine and lectureships or library appointments at Harvard and other universities. The point to be emphasized is that Thomas saw the possibility as the only real means to start afresh, and, as he put it, 'to work a lot and very much'. The output of new poems in the immediate post-war years was small, and he must have felt that the attractiveness of hack work in his impecunious condition would become increasingly dangerous to his really creative development. Though his work in films came to an end, between 1945 and 1947 he did over eighty broadcasts for the various services of the BBC. The broadcasts made him a household name, but must also have looked like swamping the time needed to write new poems. It was this imbalance in the old world which prompted him to call the new one into existence.

But before his first departure for America a new phase of creativity was to start. And in a very real sense this coincided with the poet's final move to Laugharne (in the first week of May 1949) where, within three months, a third child, Colm, was born. A final kind of settled happiness seemed possible — marred only by some financial worries (from which a man like Thomas could never in

* this visit allows authority to strip away the intimacy.

any case be free). Between his arrival in Laugharne and the first American tour of February-May 1950, he did only six broadcasts (two in any case from Wales) and worked with happy energy at new poems and at *Under Milk Wood* in the garage studio close to the now famous Boat House bought for him by Margaret Taylor and overlooking that magnificent bay and tidal beach which so clearly affected the atmosphere of his later work. The prompting of atmosphere by geography is a central aspect of the late poems. One might venture the judgement that a greater sense of community, added to this geographic rootedness, might have fruitfully widened the range of this last phase and helped to explore further the potential the poet had shown ten years before in 'After the funeral'. (The grace of hindsight again.) More important to Thomas himself, however, must have been the personal quality of wise passiveness which he was able, at least in the exercise of his art, to realize. It would be folly to suggest that the last phase was all sweetness and light: the letters of the last four years are too full of niggling financial worries and petty excuses for that. But the tonal achievements of the last poems — what Thomas in another context called 'the momentary peace which is a poem' — does point to what he himself would no doubt have considered a welcome personal maturity. There is a cruel irony in the fact that, when his recorded talk on 'Laugharne' was broadcast on 5 November 1953, it coincided with the first news in this country of his final collapse in New York. In that short talk he comically trivialized the town's character, but as a place it still measures the poet's development towards the quietus of acceptance recorded in the visionary associations of the last poems. If we look back, we see the very different mood of the younger man who had prematurely, in May 1934, spent 'Whitsun in the strangest town in Wales, Laugharne'. In 1934 he had written to Pamela Hansford Johnson, describing Laugharne sights as he saw them then:

> Each muscle in the cockler's legs is as big as a hill, and each crude footstep in the wretchedly tinted sand deep as hell. These women are sweating the oil of life out of the pores of their stupid bodies, and sweating away what brains they had so that their children might eat, be married and ravished, conceive in their wombs that are stamped with the herring, and, themselves, bring up another race of thick-lipped fools to sweat their strengths away on these unutterably deadly sands.

Even allowing for the dramatic flair which Thomas at all times showed as a correspondent, we can still see the difference between the young man of twenty and the older (though tragically still young) man who wrote the last works. That letter of 1934 could be contrasted with a poem like 'Lament' (1951) which comes through as enjoyed comedy with affinities to Yeats's 'Wild Old Wicked Man' or Louis MacNeice's 'The Libertine' and 'The Suicide'. Irreconcilable ingredients of ugliness or nastiness were now transformed into comedy or the distancing feel of myth.

It is not the purpose of an essay such as this to follow Thomas on those four tragic (yet triumphant) American trips, just as we have not followed him from pub to pub at home, and the poems of his final separate volume *In Country Sleep*, published only in America (February 1952), would be a good area in which to end. So the work which demands attention here is *Under Milk Wood*, the single work by which Thomas (unfortunately in some ways) is most widely known. And the first thing worth saying about it is that its quality is best appreciated when we concede its essentially low-key ambitions. Our appreciation is surest when we affirm that it is, quite simply, the best radio play ever written. A critic like Raymond Williams (in the *Critical Quarterly*, Spring 1959) wrote well on the play because he obviously bore its 'dramatic' modesty in mind. Conversely, David Holbrook's attack (in the *Pelican Guide to English Literature*, Vol. 7) is not so much given edge as made irrelevant by using purely literary touchstones from Joyce or T.F. Powys with which to pelt its alleged deficiencies. (It is, after all, above all else a radio 'play for voices'.) As early as 1932 Thomas had communicated to a Swansea friend, Bert Trick, his aim of writing a Welsh equivalent to *Ulysses*. But his point was only that the idea of a series of events taking the space of only twenty-four hours appealed to him; and Thomas himself had in any case often modestly confessed that Joyce's *Dubliners* sobered his assessment of his own short stories. *Under Milk Wood* is unashamedly a trivializing work in that it reduces a view of life to immediately entertaining details. We do not get anywhere with it unless we feel quite spontaneously that its jokes are relaxed and funny, and funny exactly because they are relaxed:

REV. ELI JENKINS
Oh angels be careful there with your knives and forks,

52

he prays. There is no known likeness of his father Esau, who, undogcollared because of his little weakness, was scythed to the bone one harvest by mistake when sleeping with his weakness in the corn. He lost all ambition and died, with one leg.

REV. ELI JENKINS

Poor Dad,

SECOND VOICE

grieves the Reverend Eli,

REV. ELI JENKINS

to die of drink and agriculture.

Despite the fact that the play was only really started at the end of the war, its genesis stemmed from much further back. No doubt the fantasticating imagination of the young Swansea schoolboy, as recalled in the *Portrait* story, 'Just Like Little Dogs', was a true memory:

> I was a lonely nightwalker and a steady stander-at-corners. I liked to walk through the wet town after midnight, when the streets were deserted and the window lights out, alone and alive on the glistening tramlines in dead and empty High Street under the moon, gigantically sad in the damp streets by ghostly Ebenezer Chapel.

This idea of the detached onlooker and a sleeping community is of course the basic structure of *Under Milk Wood*, and it had been exercised in Thomas's prose works from the early thirties onwards. The broadcast 'Quite Early One Morning', written for BBC Wales in 1944, was only the first formal attempt at expanding the idea. Over ten years earlier the device had been employed in the short story 'The Orchards' (1934) in which, incidentally, the word Llareggub was first used. There, some of the descriptions already looked forward to the play:

> A baby cried, but the cry grew fainter. It is all one, the loud voice and the still voice striking a common silence, the dowdy lady flattening her nose against the panes, and the well-mourned lady.

Or compare these details from the uncollected short story, 'The Horse's Ha' (1936):

53

. . . out came the grocer with an egg in his hand, and the butcher in a bloody coat . . . Butcher and baker fell asleep that night, their women sleeping at their sides . . . over the shops, the cold eggs that had life, the box where the rats worked all night on the high meat, the shopkeepers gave no thought of death.

Little lies between them and comparable details in the later 'play for voices' except disinfection of the author's earlier disaffection. Even the involvement of the audience had already been a rhetorical device in 'The Orchards':

Poor Marlais's morning, turning to evening, spins before you . . . Marlais's death in life in the circular going down of the day that had taken no time blows again in the wind for you.

David Holbrook's suggestion that this device in the play was merely a plagiarism from Eliot's 'East Coker' ('If you do not come too close, if you do not come too close') is queried in our knowledge that, for Thomas, it had been a natural legacy from way back in his own career, and also from the necessary devices of his film-scripts in the forties. The narrator-reader relationship in *The Doctor and the Devils* (1944), for example, is clearly the prototype, with camera directions like 'From our distance', 'Closer now', 'Closer still' and 'Coming closer to him'. Similarly, the freshness of the morning sequences of the play owes a lot to comparable sections in *Twenty Years A-Growing* (1944) and *The Doctor and the Devils*, just as they continued to be employed in *The Beach of Falesá* (1948, a film-script based on the short story by R.L. Stevenson). And other incidentals, such as the cataloguing of Welsh domestic items, which we have already noted in 'After the funeral' and in the story 'The Peaches', also came to a natural climax in the play.

But the poet's reading of other writers should certainly not be overlooked. If it is, we miss for example the satiric intention of a speech like this by Eli Jenkins, whose preciosity of style surely draws attention to itself even in the midst of other kinds of verbal bewitchment:

Llaregyb hill, that mystic tumulus, the memorial of peoples that dwelt in the region of Llaregyb before the Celts left the Land of Summer and where the old wizards made themselves a wife out of flowers.

Just as his hymn to the morning parodies the kind of poeticizing we find weekly in our county papers, Eli Jenkins's words at this stage derive their *frisson* from our recognition of their source not only in the story of Blodeuwedd (the girl created 'out of flowers' by the wizard Gwydion in the *Mabinogion*), but also in the perfectly 'straight' Celtic romanticism of Arthur Machen's *Autobiography* (1922): 'as soon as I saw anything I saw Twyn Barlwm, that mystic tumulus, the memorial of the peoples that dwelt in that region before the Celts left the Land of Summer.' Thomas's 'play for voices' appears a little less soft-centred when we note these satiric anti-romantic touches. Another example would be the First Voice's leg-pull when he says,

> The music of the spheres is heard distinctly over Milk Wood. It is 'The Rustle of Spring'.

It helps if we know that 'The Rustle of Spring', by the Norwegian composer Sinding, was a salon piece which carried 'best room' connotations of static ordinariness through being a cliché of bourgeois musical taste. And how long, we wonder, had Thomas known the American Edgar Lee Masters' *Spoon River Anthology* (1915)? He wrote a penetrating essay in introduction to a radio reading of selections from that work in September 1952, when he was revising *Under Milk Wood*. The parallels between the two works are obvious. In Masters' series of free-verse poems, the dead of the town of Spoon River speak from the graveyard of the fears, loves and wants that had driven them in life; and the Epilogue, of course, has the dramatic structure of Thomas's play, complete with First and Second Voices. At least as safe a bet is that the marvellous drowned sailors' sequence in the play owed something directly to Thomas Hardy's poems, 'Friends Beyond' and 'Voices From Things Growing In A Churchyard'. The point is that Thomas, in writing the play, was spontaneously amalgamating several ingredients from his own and others' writings. With direct experience of communities like New Quay and Laugharne itself, the play was a naturally relaxed and impressionistic venture. The whole was held together as if shaped by natural impulses of language and style. The main characteristics of that style even carried over into his description of the play in his letters.

This is not to say that the work was speedily executed. The writing of *Under Milk Wood* was fantastically protracted. Thomas, quite dishonestly, sold it twice in an unfinished state. A section of it appeared, as 'Llareggub: A Piece For Radio Perhaps', in the international magazine, *Botteghe Oscure*, in April 1952. During the third American tour (April–June 1953) it was read in an unfinished state several times, at Harvard and at the Poetry Center of the Young Men and Young Women's Hebrew Association in New York (of which John Malcolm Brinnin was Director) with Thomas adding material up to the last minute. But these readings especially must at least have reassured him of the work's obvious appeal.

In a sense, there was even a philosophical urgency of sorts behind the work. Its conscious genesis lay perhaps in the December of 1939, when the poet told Richard Hughes the novelist (and a neighbour — Hughes lived in a house in the grounds of Laugharne Castle) that 'what the people of Laugharne need is a play about themselves, a play in which they can act themselves'. The idea of those depicted being also the actors was an interesting one, basic as it was at one time to the tradition of the Masque; and when staged, the play, it seems to me, still has an extra dimension when the actors are not out-and-out professionals. Certainly, effortful pseudo-Welsh performances tend to fail. But to return to the point: when Thomas further described the plot to Richard Hughes, in about 1943, and again to Constantine FitzGibbon at the end of the war, when news of Hitler's concentration camps was current, he had developed the idea of the village community being an island of eccentric innocence in an insane world. With this over-emphasis, the structure was perhaps a little grotesque, with the village officially condemned as mad by an inspector from the outside world (although wittily willing to accept that verdict simply because the outside world seemed so insane!). But a reminder of that previous structure helps at least to highlight the play's character as a version of pastoral. Withdrawal from the world equalled a retreat into sanity. In the end this is where its strength lies.

The uncanny sense we have — while recognizing *Under Milk Wood* as in many other ways an unpretentious sport — that some kind of imaginative truth still holds good in our experience of it, comes from the way in which it ministers to a concept of basic innocence. Where this issues to the surface in the speech of characters — Polly Garter's

> Isn't life a terrible thing, thank God

or Eli Jenkins's

> We are not wholly bad or good —

it is of course only partly convincing as moral judgement. But a more real persuasiveness lies in the play's subtle use of pastoral, visionary tones. Mary Ann Sailors, for example,

> goes down the cockleshelled paths of that applepie kitchen garden, ducking under the gippo's clothespegs, catching her apron on the blackcurrant bushes, past beanrows and onion-bed and tomatoes ripening on the wall towards the old man playing the harmonium in the orchard, and sits down on the grass at his side and shells the green peas that grow up through the lap of her frock that brushes the dew.

The radio medium enabled Thomas once again to soft-pedal the difficulties he might have found in providing a stiffer, more challenging, dramatic structure — and enabled him to live once again, as one side of him was always tempted to do, in a world of words. Some of the subtler pastoral shades made possible by its being a 'play for voices' are lost in a stage production. The play does not call us to any coldly literary response, to any orthodoxly dramatic involvement, and certainly not to any serious kind of sociological estimate of the nature of Welsh society. To some degree, it is natural that the important renaissance of Welsh cultural nationalist pride in the decades since Thomas's death has caused resentment at what might seem this free-trading in 'stage-Welshness', but that resentment could clearly not be of the same proportion or intensity as that manifested by the Irishmen who, as Yeats put it, hated Synge's *Playboy of the Western World* in 1907. And, anyway, a final truce seems to have been signed across the language-barrier in the translation of the play into Welsh, as *Dan y Wenallt*. Every aspect of *Under Milk Wood* is suggested in the ease with which it has become something of an innocuous classic.

In a BBC broadcast of September 1950 called 'Three Poems', Thomas introduced 'In Country Sleep' (1947), 'Over Sir John's hill' (1949) and 'In the White Giant's Thigh' (1950) as parts of a

long poem which he was going to call 'In Country Heaven'. The
scheme under which they were to be linked sounds at first as fantastic
as 'The Town is Mad' idea of the 'play for voices'. In 'In Country
Heaven', God and the inhabitants of Country Heaven would learn of
the atomic extinction of Earth. Country Heaven suddenly goes dark,
and those inhabitants who were once of the Earth call to each other
through the darkness their memories of that place:

> They remember places, fears, loves, exultation, misery, animal joy,
> ignorance, and mysteries, all we know and do not know.

As with the play, the poems themselves seem relatively innocent of
their philosophic cover-note: the rationalized structure of the
composite whole was not allowed to disturb the lyric business of the
individual poems. The structure itself was certainly not an
explorative one. The unfinished title-poem 'In Country Heaven'
(evolved slowly between 1947 and 1951) looks as if it was meant to
be merely situational, in effect a verse rendering of the explanation
of the broadcast. The poet's tone in that 1950 broadcast was
essentially tentative, even self-deprecating:

> What can I say about this long poem-to-be except that the plan of it is
> grand and simple and that the grandeur will seem, to many, to be
> purple and grandiose and the simplicity crude and sentimental?

But his imaginative commitment inside each of the three individual
poems that were meant to be subsumed in the overall plan bears out
his claim that the composite production of 'In Country Heaven'
was aimed at an accumulation of 'praise of what is and what could
be on this lump in the skies. It is a poem about happiness.'

In this way, all Thomas's late poems finally confirm and embody
his matured sense that the only response to experience of which he
is capable is that of affirmative acceptance. In early poems such as
'Where once the waters of your face' or 'Our eunuch dreams', this
quality of affirmation had been rather vulnerably a matter of final-
stanza optimism:

celebration
that the
'is meant'
is subsumed
is yet to
yet to
world

> And we shall be fit fellows for a life,
> And who remain shall flower as they love,
> Praise to our faring hearts.

> ('Our eunuch dreams')

58

Now, at the end of the career, the affirmation is manifested in the descriptive texture of the whole poem. A quality of assertive praise links him now not only to heterodox Blake but also to orthodox Hopkins, in a way which makes the poems' own occasional summary gestures — 'A hill touches an angel' or 'The country is holy' — seem almost self-consciously redundant. 'Over Sir John's hill', for example, does not excite us because of any paraphrasable quantity: indeed, its final line — 'for the sake of the souls of the slain birds sailing' — seems to push its emblematic significance for man dangerously close to a detachable, and therefore a debatable, explicitness. (In what sense, we might retort, do birds have souls?) But the real strength of 'Over Sir John's hill', like that of Hopkins's 'The Windhover', lies in the fact that it is all the while engaging on a tonal, descriptive level. Such poems are, first of all, events. Thomas's affirmative strength in these late poems lies in his ability (at times also a Hardy-like ability) to create impressions of life and energy in the face of unignorable death. A good example would be the childless women buried on the hill in 'In the White Giant's Thigh', who once

> gay with anyone
> Young as they in the after milking moonlight lay
>
> Under the lighted shapes of faith and their moonshade
> Petticoats galed high, or shy with the rough riding boys,
> Now clasp me to their grains in the gigantic glade,
>
> Who once, green countries since, were a hedgerow of joys.

'In the White Giant's Thigh' (1949) shows that the possibilities so eminently suggested in 'After the funeral' back in 1938 were still open to him, that he could have continued to act as the sad historian of a Welsh pastoral community, in ways which would have exercised increasingly rewarding demands on his instinctive place-consciousness.

But as it happens, the greater emphasis in the late poems is thrown onto the poet's own spiritual condition. Urging his sleeping daughter to accept his assurance of a 'designed', 'true', 'sure', 'shaped' and 'ruled' universe (the key words in the final lines of 'In Country Sleep'), he is of course firstly convincing himself. Incidentally, for 'ruled' Thomas had originally written 'chained', reminding us of the paradox of 'Fern Hill''s final line. 'Over Sir John's hill' likewise communicates, without distress or palliation, the straightforward fact of death: the victory comes in seeing it straight. Allowing of course for the obvious differences in style, Yeats's battlings with remorse and his celebration of a tragic gaiety come to mind.

Thomas's religious position has been the topic of much discussion, and various formulations have been offered, from Empson's 'pessimistic pantheism' or FitzGibbon's suggestion of something like a reluctant agnosticism through to Aneirin Talfan Davies's bid to make Thomas all but a Catholic. One thing which seems certain is that we ought not to place the poet inside any orthodoxy. That the poems are often full of a wide range of quite orthodox allusions has only a limited significance. The received Christian framework is often an imagistic means whereby we provide ourselves, in ordinary conversation as much as in creative work, with a structure for thought — and without which, in certain imaginative contexts, we cannot think at all. In the absence of a Christian persuasion, a poet like Yeats created his own intellectual frameworks for his poems, occult and often freakish. Dylan Thomas, with a resistance, as we have seen, to any kind of dogmatic conclusiveness, nevertheless accepted a tradition whose images, and indeed some of whose insights, he found to be congenial as poet and man. Reared in a society whose local, puritanical version of that Christian tradition must have struck him as having more to do with negative control of secular activity than with any penetration of the numinous — and deeply affected throughout his life by the free-thinking pessimism of his father — he had had a leeway to make up which was not spanned by any firm theological development. But it is not necessarily a criticism to say that his career was the refinement, not of belief, but of the emotions.

His final position is that poignantly recorded in 'Poem on his Birthday' which was completed in July 1951 and which, like 'Over Sir John's hill' and so many others of his works, exults in its Laugharne location. 'In the mustardseed sun', he says,

> By full tilt river and switchback sea
> Where the cormorants scud,
> In his house on stilts high among beaks
> And palavers of birds

he is caught between the natural urge to describe and celebrate, and the frustration of not having any fixed and quieting belief of orthodox proportions to contain those celebratory instincts:

> And freely he goes lost
> In the unknown, famous light of great
> And fabulous, dear God.
> Dark is a way and light is a place,
> Heaven that never was
> Nor will be ever is always true . . .

His own thirty-five years (the poem was presumably begun in 1949), and the animal activity of his location, present again the facts of mortality. Unlike the herons or the rippled seals, or the flounders and gulls 'doing what they are told', he himself does not have the advantage of being able only unconsciously to fulfil natural function. Perhaps we can best hit off his predicament by once again deflecting our attention for a moment to the comparable situation Keats found himself in when he wrote his journal-letter to his brother in February-May 1819:

> Very few men have ever arrived at a complete disinterestedness of Mind: very few have been influenced by a pure desire of the benefit of others — in the greater part of the Benefactors (of) and to Humanity some meretricious motive has sullied their greatness — some melodramatic scenery has fascinated them — in wild nature the hawk would loose his Breakfast of Robins and the Robin his of Worms . . . The greater part of Men make their way with the same instinctiveness, the same unwandering eye from their purposes, the same animal eagerness as the Hawk . . . I go among the Fields and catch a glimpse of a stoat or a fieldmouse peeping out of the withered grass — the creature hath a purpose and its eyes are bright with it . . . there is an electric fire in human nature tending to purify — so that among these human creatures there is continually some birth of new heroism — The pity is that we must wonder at it: as we should at finding a pearl in rubbish . . . Even here though I myself am pursuing the same instinctive course as the veriest human animal you can think of — I am however young writing at random — straining at particles of light in the midst of a great darkness — without knowing the bearing of any one assertion of any one opinion. Yet may I not in this be free from sin?

'Yet may I not in this be free from sin?' It is this same assertion of innocence in the face of ideological blankness that animates

Thomas's poem, and it has more to do with the need to win through to a sense of general optimism than with any specific creed. Without Eliot's actual theology, Thomas comes near on a minor level to the purpose of the *Four Quartets* — an acceptance of Time through a simultaneous awareness, within it, of the Timeless. If the *Four Quartets* ever exerted an actual influence, however, that influence went into some of the imagery of Thomas's final poems. Eliot's 'The Dry Salvages', for example — 'The starfish, the horse-shoe crab, the whale's backbone' — is brought to mind in the seventh stanza of 'Poem on his Birthday':

> There he might wander bare
> With the spirits of the horseshoe bay
> Or the stars' seashore dead,
> Marrow of eagles, the roots of whales
> And wishbones of wild geese.

Or 'Little Gidding' —

> Dust inbreathed was a house —
> The wall, the wainscot and the mouse —

in 'In the White Giant's Thigh':

> The dust of their kettles and clocks swings to and fro
> Where the hay rides now or the bracken kitchens rust.

Thomas's final poems attempt to merge and submerge personal elegy in an awareness of a more general mortality whose pattern is not annihilation but change. If they illustrate any technical danger, it is that of too much verbal glamour. But as a climax to this particular career they have their own logic and their own kind of honesty.

The summer of 1951, because in the first place his London visits were few, was the poet's last productive period. His final three years were otherwise disrupted by the logical consequences of his four American visits (February–June 1950, January–May 1952, April–June and October–November 1953). Because of his real and imagined indiscretions on those tours, his relations with his wife were strained, often close to breaking point. Thomas's financial incompetence in America, plus the increasing attention of the

Inland Revenue at home, meant also that the fantastic monetary reward for those trips — reckoned in thousands of dollars — was never allowed to help his domestic stability at home. As always, and in all things, he was his own worst enemy. In such conditions, almost as soon as one tour was over the next one had to be considered. (In between the first and second American visits he also went to Persia to make a documentary film, subsequently cancelled, for the Anglo-Iranian Oil Company.) Caitlin insisted on accompanying him on the second American tour early in 1952, but she failed to make its financial profitability any better, and the Inland Revenue was now claiming a staggering £1,607 on the disappeared earnings of the first visit. The gap in literary productivity, however, was minimized by Dent's wise decision to publish, in November 1952, a *Collected Poems 1934–1952*, for which Thomas spent a whole year writing his 'Prologue' in verse, to the exclusion of any other poem. The volume consolidated, to the different amazement of admirers and detractors, the nature and scope of the poet's achievement over two decades. It prompted the award of the Foyle's Poetry Prize; and, selling 30,000 copies in the British edition alone in 1953–4, it promised financial rewards which Dylan Thomas himself never lived to receive. Nevertheless, despite the fact that certain fears and logical consequences were coming home to roost, and that his father died blind and in pain a month after the publication of *Collected Poems*, the pointers at the time were towards a challenging future, symbolized chiefly in the projected collaboration with Stravinsky in the writing of an opera. But Thomas was tired and obviously ill, and the pattern of American lecture and reading tours could be neither avoided nor survived. On 9 November 1953 he died in St Vincent's Hospital in New York City.

A Selected Bibliography

DYLAN THOMAS

J. Alexander Rolph's *Dylan Thomas: A Bibliography* (1956) has been superseded by Ralph Maud's *Dylan Thomas in Print: A Bibliographical History* (Pittsburgh, University of Pittsburgh Press, 1970; London, Dent, 1972 with an appendix by Walford Davies).

Collected Poems 1934–1953 (London, Dent, 1988). The definitive edition, edited by Walford Davies and Ralph Maud.

Poet in the Making: The Notebooks of Dylan Thomas (London, Dent, 1968), edited with an introduction by Ralph Maud. Second edition, revised, 1989 (as *Dylan Thomas: The Notebook Poems 1930–1934*).

Portrait of the Artist as a Young Dog (London, Dent, 1940).

The Doctor and the Devils (London, Dent, 1953).

Under Milk Wood: 'A Play for Voices' (London, Dent, 1954).

Quite Early One Morning: Broadcasts by Dylan Thomas (London, Dent, 1954) with a preface by Aneirin Talfan Davies.

A Prospect of the Sea and other Stories and Prose Writings (London, Dent, 1955), edited by Daniel Jones.

Adventures in the Skin Trade (London, Putnam, 1955) with a foreword by Vernon Watkins.

Letters to Vernon Watkins (London, Dent, 1957), edited with an introduction by Vernon Watkins.

The Beach of Falesá (London, Jonathan Cape, 1963). Film-script based on Robert Louis Stevenson's short story.

Twenty Years A-Growing (London, Dent, 1964). Film-script based on the story by Maurice O'Sullivan.

Dylan Thomas: Early Prose Writings (London, Dent, 1971), edited with an introduction by Walford Davies. Includes early short stories previously uncollected.

The Collected Letters of Dylan Thomas (London, Dent, 1985), edited by Paul Ferris.

Biography

John Malcolm Brinnin, *Dylan Thomas in America: An Intimate Journal* (London, Dent, 1956).

Caitlin Thomas, *Leftover Life to Kill* (London, Putnam, 1957).

Bill Read, *The Days of Dylan Thomas* (London, Weidenfeld and Nicolson, 1965), with photographs by Rollie McKenna and others.

Constantine FitzGibbon, *The Life of Dylan Thomas* (London, Dent, 1965).

Paul Ferris, *Dylan Thomas* (London, Hodder and Stoughton, 1977).

Caitlin Thomas with George Tremlett, *Caitlin: Life with Dylan Thomas* (London, Secker and Warburg, 1986).

Criticism

Henry Treece, *Dylan Thomas: 'Dog Among the Fairies'* (London, Lindsay Drummond, 1949. Revised 1956).

Derek Stanford, *Dylan Thomas: A Literary Study* (London, Neville Spearman, 1954).

G.S. Fraser, *Dylan Thomas* ('Writers and their Work' Series for the British Council) (London, Longmans, Green, 1957).

E.W. Tedlock (ed.), *Dylan Thomas: The Legend and the Poet* (London, Heinemann, 1960). A collection of biographical and critical essays.

David Holbrook, *Llareggub Revisited: Dylan Thomas and the State of Modern Poetry* (London, Bowes and Bowes, 1962).

Claude Rawson, *Dylan Thomas (Talks to Teachers of English 2)* (Newcastle upon Tyne, Department of Education, King's College, 1962).

W.Y. Tindall, *A Reader's Guide to Dylan Thomas* (London, Thames and Hudson, 1962).

T.H. Jones, *Dylan Thomas* ('Writers and Critics' Series) (Edinburgh and London, 1963).

Ralph Maud, *Entrances to Dylan Thomas' Poetry* (Lowestoft, Scorpion Press, 1963).

John Ackerman, *Dylan Thomas: His Life and Work* (London, Oxford University Press, 1964).

Aneirin Talfan Davies, *Dylan: Druid of the Broken Body* (London, Dent, 1964).

C.B. Cox (ed.), *Dylan Thomas: A Collection of Critical Essays* ('Twentieth Century Views' Series) (Englewood Cliffs, New Jersey, Prentice-Hall, 1966).

W.T. Moynihan, *The Craft and Art of Dylan Thomas* (London, Oxford University Press, 1966).

Walford Davies (ed.), *Dylan Thomas: New Critical Essays* (London, Dent, 1972).

David Holbrook, *Dylan Thomas and the Code of Night* (London, The Athlone Press, University of London, 1972).

John Ackerman, *Welsh Dylan* (Cardiff, John Jones, 1979).

Walford Davies, *Dylan Thomas* ('Open Guides to Literature' Series) (Milton Keynes, Open University Press, 1986).

John Ackerman, *The Dylan Thomas Companion* (London, Macmillan Press, 1990).

Books on wider topics which contain valuable essays on Dylan Thomas include:

John Bayley, *The Romantic Survival: A Study in Poetic Evolution* (London, Constable, 1957). Chapter 10, 'Dylan Thomas', is an outstanding critical essay.

Winifred Nowottny, *The Language Poets Use* (London, The Athlone Press, University of London, 1962). Chapter 8 gives a detailed explication of 'There was a saviour'.

J. Hillis Miller, *Poets of Reality: Six Twentieth-Century Writers* (London, Oxford University Press, 1966). Chapter 5 is on Dylan Thomas.

Laurence Lerner, *The Uses of Nostalgia* (London, Chatto and Windus, 1972). Includes a valuable essay on *Under Milk Wood* as a form of pastoral. A version of this material also appears in Walford Davies (ed.), *Dylan Thomas: New Critical Essays*, above.

The Author

Professor Walford Davies is Director of the Department of Extra-Mural Studies at the University College of Wales, Aberystwyth, where he also holds a personal chair in English Literature. He was formerly Senior Lecturer in English Literature at St Anne's College, Oxford. A native of Pontyberem, Carmarthenshire, he was educated at Gwendraeth Grammar School and Keble College, Oxford. He edited *Dylan Thomas: Early Prose Writings* (Dent, 1971) and *Dylan Thomas: New Critical Essays* (Dent, 1972), and is the author of *Dylan Thomas* (Open University Press, 1986). He has edited the poetry of Wordsworth, Gerard Manley Hopkins, and Thomas Hardy. With Professor Ralph Maud, he is co-editor of the definitive edition of Dylan Thomas's *Collected Poems 1934–1953* (Dent, 1988). He is currently completing a critical study of the poetry of Gerard Manley Hopkins. Walford Davies is married, with two sons.